LIVING IN STYLE

~

WITHOUT LOSING YOUR MIND

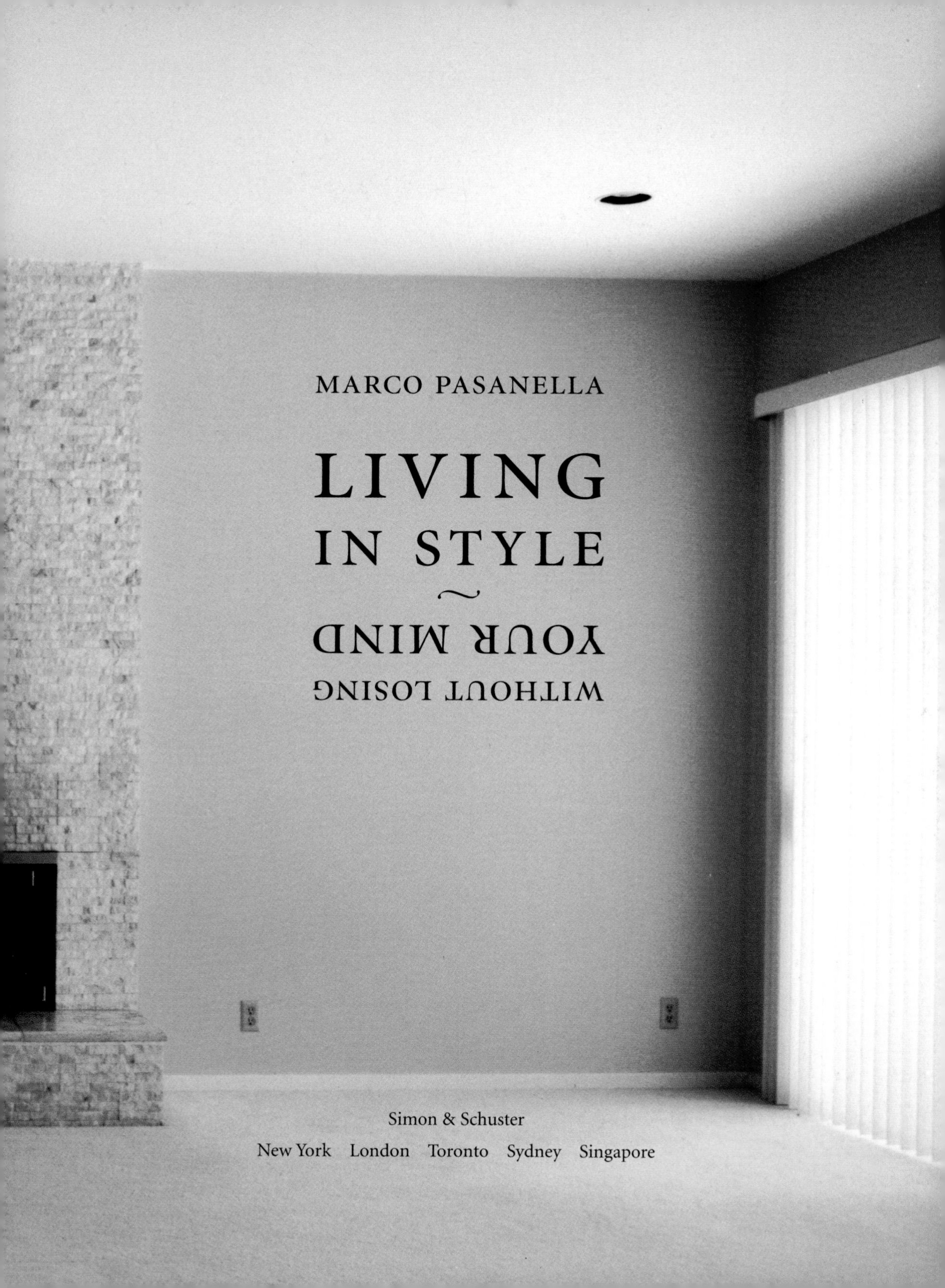

MARCO PASANELLA

LIVING IN STYLE ~ WITHOUT LOSING YOUR MIND

Simon & Schuster

New York London Toronto Sydney Singapore

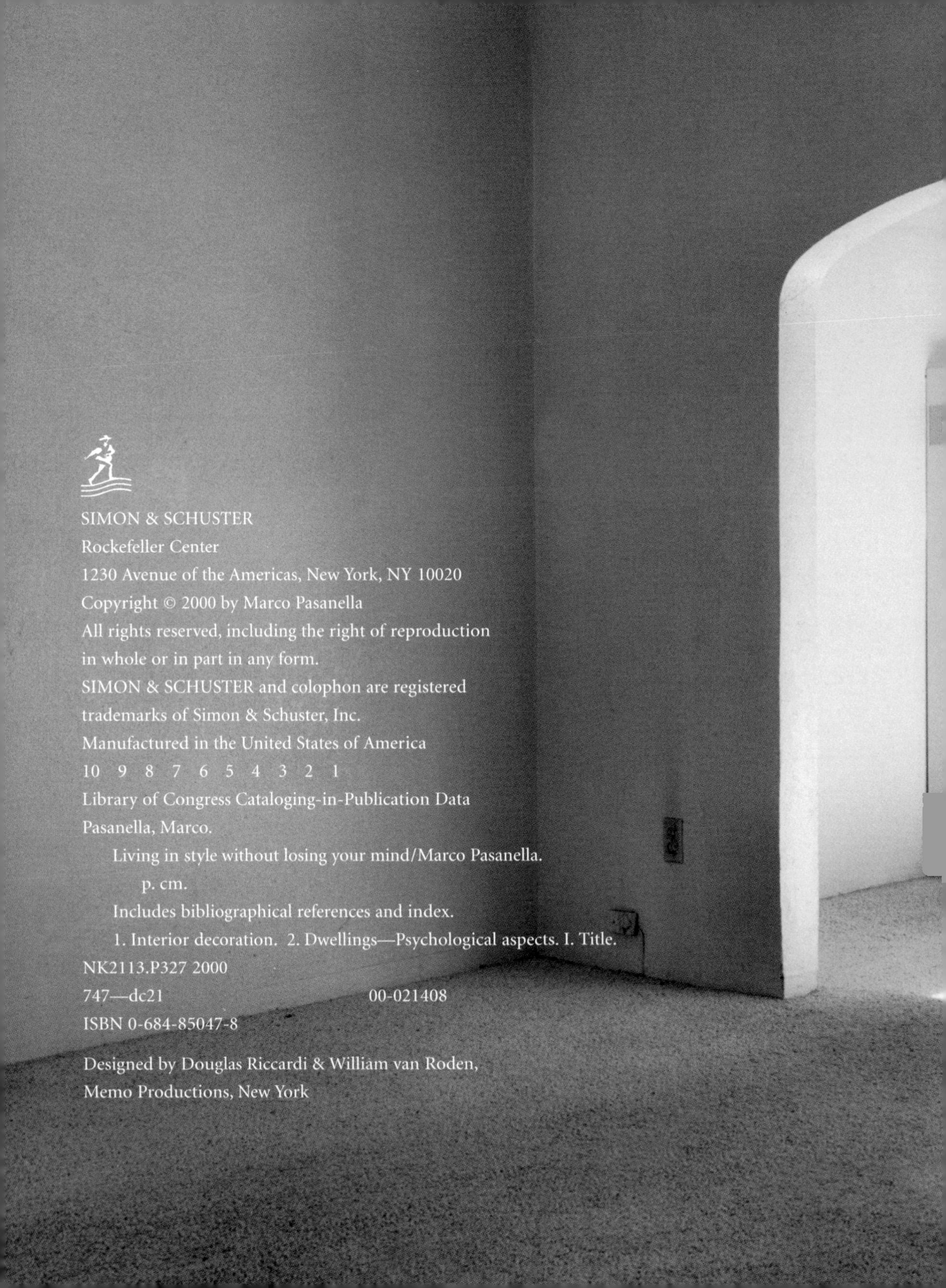

SIMON & SCHUSTER
Rockefeller Center
1230 Avenue of the Americas, New York, NY 10020

Manufactured in the United States of America
10 9 8 7 6 5 4 3 2 1
Library of Congress Cataloging-in-Publication Data
Pasanella, Marco.
Living in style without losing your mind/Marco Pasanella.
p. cm.
Includes bibliographical references and index.
1. Interior decoration. 2. Dwellings—Psychological aspects. I. Title.
NK2113.P327 2000
747—dc21 00-021408
ISBN 0-684-85047-8

Designed by Douglas Riccardi & William van Roden,
Memo Productions, New York

TO MY FATHER

WHO TAUGHT ME TO SEE

AND TO MY MOTHER

WHO TAUGHT ME HOW TO LISTEN

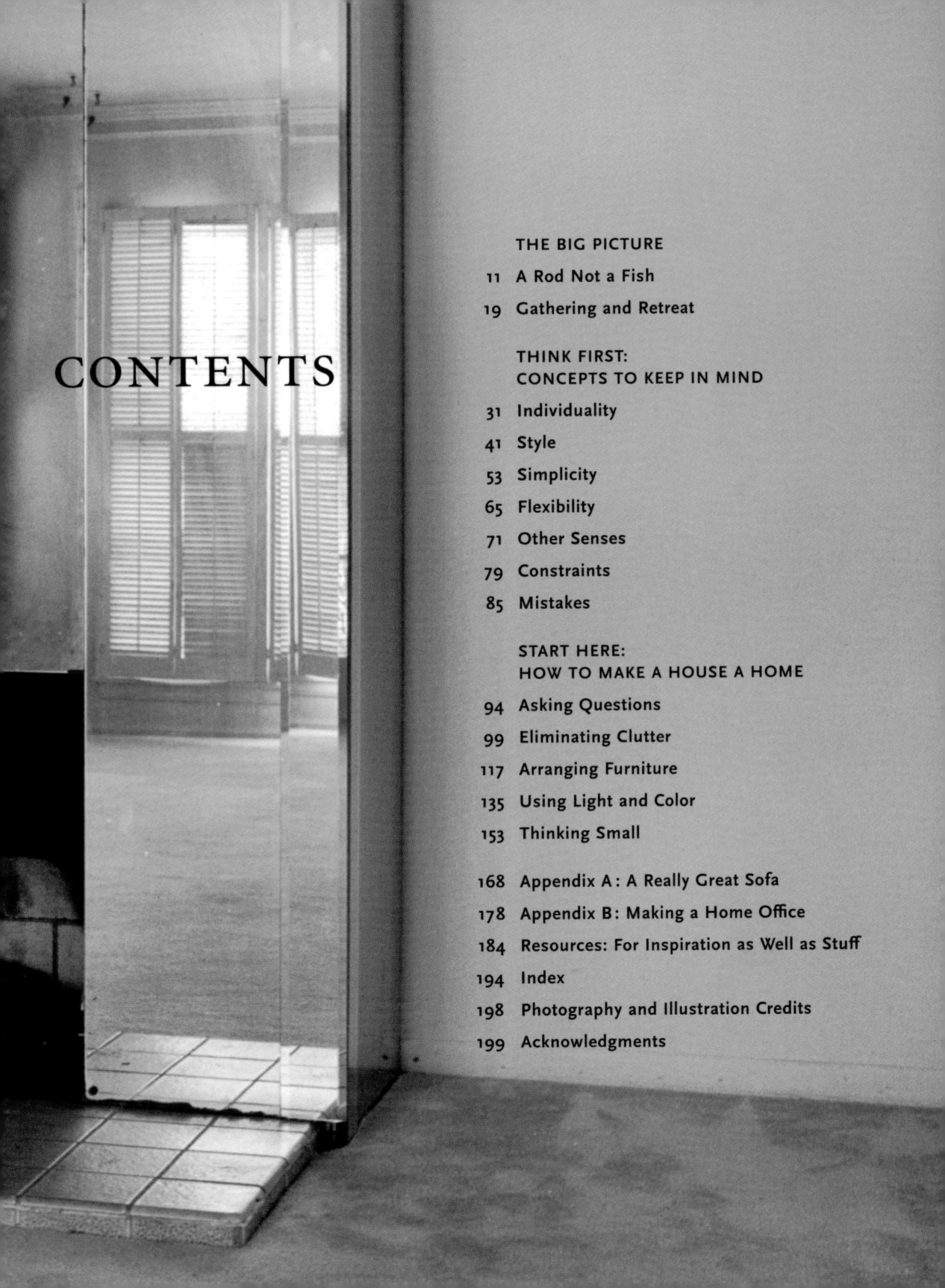

CONTENTS

THE BIG PICTURE

Sicilian room and boy.

A ROD NOT A FISH

IN THE PEACE CORPS, THEY SAY THAT IT IS BETTER TO TEACH A MAN TO FISH THAN TO GIVE HIM ONE. TO BE INDEPENDENT, THE REASONING GOES, YOU HAVE TO LEARN TO FISH FOR YOURSELF. TO MAKE CHOICES, YOU HAVE TO GRASP THEM. UNFORTUNATELY, TOO MANY DESIGNERS' BOOKS JUST OFFER FISH. Fine, if you live how they live, where they live, with their stuff; but not so good if you want a home that reflects you. This book, on the other hand, is for people who want to understand rather than imitate.

The first step is to know what you're aiming for.

You may want your home to look like a magazine, but to do so may require a mountain of money and a staff of hundreds, the dexterity of Michelangelo, and a backhoe. But for that kind of cash, labor, and expertise, it better be pretty damn great (see the Piazza San Marco).

Most of the time (almost all the time, in fact) great design has to be accessible to the rest of us. By definition, it has to be easy

My home is at least three rooms and a terrace short of perfect. But what this small apartment lacks in pyrotechnics, it makes up in personal resonance. I love it for all the things you'd never notice in a magazine: for an unfortunate picture taken moments after my birth. For an apple-picking ladder that draws attention to the high ceiling. For my trophy goldfish, stuffed and mounted on the mantel.

and affordable, smart and stylish. But you don't need a "look." Rather, based on a point of view, great design can be found in many styles.

All design is composed, to varying degrees, of the following elements: space, form, light, color, material, scale, and symbols (or associations). Good design gets the mix right; but great design includes one more: passion. You don't appreciate great design; you love it. Great design describes inanimate things (objects, spaces) that inspire human attachment. It's personal. It resonates. It enthralls. Truly great design is what you would carry out of your house if it were burning down.

In a world where everything is starting to look like everything else (think Pottery Barn, Crate & Barrel, Williams-Sonoma) great design is a little off. It includes the unpolished, the unique, perhaps even the slightly nutty. To have great design, you've got to have a little something, with a little something extra.

Design can be scary. It seems to involve spending a lot of money, taking a lot of time, and making a lot of seemingly arbi-

TO HAVE A GREAT HOME, THE POINT IS,
YOU DON'T NEED A PLATINUM CARD FOR A FLAIR FOR FABRICS.
YOU NEED TO KNOW HOW TO *SEE*.

trary decisions. It doesn't have to. All you need to do is understand how to recognize it for yourself. To have a great home, the point is, you don't need a platinum card for a flair for fabrics. You don't need a degree. You don't even need to know how to draw. You need to know how to *see*. And this book will show you how.

Sometimes that means looking not in a Sotheby's catalog but in places closer to home. Great design, one should keep in mind, is often so well designed as not to seem designed at all.

Often it just means remembering.

Everything you need to know about design you learned in freshman English, at least if you read William Strunk and E. B. White's *Elements of Style* as you were supposed to. On close examination, this guide to good writing gives some brilliant advice about good design. "Work from a suitable design," Strunk and White advise. Do the same at home. Decide what's important and go about it in a methodical way. "This does not mean," they sensibly point out, "that you must sit with a blueprint always in front of you, merely that you had best anticipate what you are getting into."

The shelf at the end of this twelve-foot ladder keeps cookies out of easy reach.

The practical doesn't have to compromise the personal. This rack in my kitchen holds pots as well as pictures.

Keep it simple, the authors continue: "A sentence should contain no unnecessary words, a paragraph no unnecessary sentences, for the same reasons that a drawing should have no unnecessary lines and a machine no unnecessary parts. This requires not that the writer make all his sentences short, or that he avoid all detail and treat his subject only in outline, but that every word tell."

"Approach style warily," they wisely caution. Turn "resolutely away from all devices that are popularly believed to indicate style—all mannerisms, tricks, adornments." Remember that style is what is "distinguished and distinguishing," not a "garnish for the meat of prose, a sauce by which a dull dish can be made palatable." Once again, the same is true for interior design. Style is important. *A* style is not.

Heed *Elements of Style* and you'll realize that the ability to make a home look great is neither a mystical talent nor a God-given blessing bestowed upon a lucky few. Interior design has principles, and the most fundamental of these are gathering and retreat.

Dinnertime, Tashkent, Uzbekistan.

GATHERING AND RETREAT

WHETHER YOU LIVE IN A MANSION OR IN A STUDIO, IN BOSTON OR IN BALI, THERE ARE ONLY TWO TYPES OF ROOMS: THOSE THAT BRING US TOGETHER (GATHERING PLACES) AND THOSE THAT ALLOW US TO GET AWAY (RETREATS). GATHERING PLACES INCLUDE LIVING ROOMS, DINING ROOMS, KITCHENS, AND, ORIGINALLY, BONFIRES. According to historian Joseph Rykwert, architecture was created to mimic the comfort of gathering around a flame. Like a roaring fire, every great room has a focus. At home, this center derives from how you arrange the furniture.

While a bonfire is visually hypnotic, a fire's stimulation of other senses also contributes to its ability to bring us together. Like our desire for heat. A cozy room is like a hot fire. It invites nesting. We tend to gather around heat sources, whether fireplaces and wood-burning stoves or lapdogs and loved ones.

Gathering started around a fire. Even today, few elements help us come together better than a roaring flame (although a good coffee table, *opposite,* usually does the trick).

In the summer, the opposite is true—we seek out screened-in porches and airy loggias—but the principle remains the same: people tend to cluster in the most desirable climate, even if it's just a corner of a room.

Materials also strongly influence how we gather. Just as soft grass beats a wet cave, so are we more liable to settle on a plump down cushion than on a chilly marble floor. Even sound plays a role. A fire's crackle, for example, draws us in.

More than giving us something to huddle around, good homes and big bonfires also draw us together by allowing for a lot of informal contact. Fires invite us to grab a rock or a patch of ground to sit where we want. Similarly, an inviting house gives guests equally many choices of where and how to gather. Their

layouts recognize that the most well-used areas are not often what they are supposed to be; that we are less likely to plunk down in a formal dining room than in some comfortable spot in between the door and an official sitting area. More discoveries than destinations, these casual stopping points are crucial to comfortable living spaces.

One of the most powerful elements encouraging people to come together doesn't seem like a "design" topic, but it's more effective than anything you will ever do with wallpaper. Simply put, we tend to hang out where we eat. Substitute nachos for spit-roasted boar and the effect is the same. That may mean gathering in the dining room, but more often it's in the kitchen, around the coffee table, or wherever you happen to place the dip.

Writer Henry David Thoreau's
cabin is the archetypal retreat.

Get the furniture right and the colors ideal, and you're on the way to a perfect *space*, a stage set for living. But the point is, what you want is the perfect *place*. To really make a house a home, you've got to have people over.

Mao Zedong's bedroom hideaway.

A PLACE TO RETREAT

Every home must provide a place to get away. This area may be a study, a bedroom, or just a bathroom, but all of them have to allow you to dream.

The archetypal retreat, in America at least, is Henry David Thoreau's famous cabin on Walden Pond. Built in 1845, the 9' x 15' cottage is small, even by today's squished standards. Most things are within an arm's reach; the door is only slightly taller than one's head. But for a single person, the cozy size is ideal. The rustic dwelling is just big enough to allow for privacy. As Thoreau put it: "I would rather sit alone on a pumpkin than crowded on a velvet cushion."

Similarly, at home, everyone needs a room of one's own—even if it's just an alcove. As architectural theorist Christopher Alexander points out: "No one can be close to others without also having frequent opportunities to be alone."

Part of the appeal of Thoreau's one-room shack is not just its size but its simplicity. Convinced that most houses were "cluttered and defiled" with furniture, he advised that a "good house-

wife would sweep the better part into a dust hole." Thoreau's own spartan retreat is made of $28 worth of old boards, used shingles, and little else. Its beauty, Thoreau contended, came from having evolved to conform to its inhabitant. Not so much constructed as patched together, the Walden cabin is imperfect, unintimidating. It makes you feel comfortable.

Admittedly, part of this shack's appeal also comes from its sylvan setting in the Massachusetts woods, but many retreats share this direct connection to the outdoors. George Bernard Shaw's studio, for example, was mounted on a huge lazy Susan, allowing it to rotate with the sun. Like Thoreau's cabin, Shaw's writing cottage soothes the body as it stimulates the mind. By keeping the elements at bay, both refuges are great examples of what one writer has called "shelters for the imagination."

But retreats aren't necessarily so placid. And they definitely aren't predicated on scented candles. The true measure of any getaway, in fact, lies in its ability to inspire. And sometimes the most inspired ones are a little crazy.

Kurt Schwitters, the well-known Dada artist, spent sixteen years constructing his ideal retreat out of paper. The *Merzbau,* as he called it, became a huge three-dimensional collage, a kind of walk-in artwork that was anything but monastic. Too bad it burned down. Jackson Pollock also had an exciting hideaway where, in addition to dripping paint everywhere, he smoked,

A retreat doesn't need to be a whole room. Sometimes it can be a nook or even a tent.

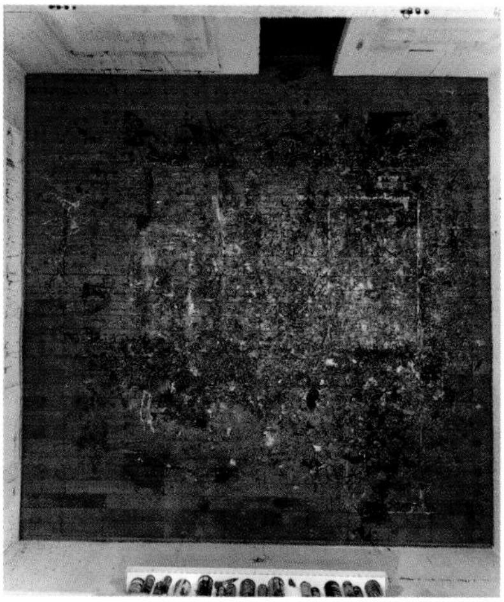

A good retreat doesn't have to be dull, as Jackson Pollock realized.

Opposite: Bathrooms are natural refuges, rooms that provide solace and serenity.

drank, and, according to scholars, cursed a lot. Your home's retreat may be more prosaic—a terry-covered chair in the bathroom, a window seat and a favorite book, a garage—but it must have at least one place that allows you to dream.

That's the big picture: the goal (understanding great design), the method (a lot of critical thinking and a little madness), and the underlying dynamic (gathering and retreat). The following chapters tell you what to keep in mind and then how to go about transforming that Pier 1 fire sale into a dream home.

By the end, if you put these principles into action, your living space should be comfortable and beautiful. But beware: it will not be "done." "Done" is not the goal. Instead, your home should feel eminently livable and aesthetically pleasing but it should be able to accommodate change without messing up some grand scheme. Your home should evolve with you. Hopefully, this book will help as much with these incremental changes ("Where's the best place to put that great new chair?") as with the big challenges ("Where do I put the new baby?").

THINK FIRST

CONCEPTS TO KEEP IN MIND

Man and Vespa, Naples.

INDIVIDUALITY

IF GREAT DESIGN DEPENDS ON PASSION, THEN INDIVIDUALITY IS THE KEY. YOUR HOME HAS TO BE PERSONAL. IT HAS TO REFLECT WHO YOU ARE. YOUR LIFESTYLE, YOUR INTERESTS, YOUR OBSESSIONS. THE BEST-DESIGNED SPACES MIRROR THEIR OWNERS, IDIOSYNCRASIES AND ALL. BUT DON'T GET THE WRONG IDEA. Individual isn't kooky. Crazy-looking homes are often the manic products of insecure people who desperately want to be interesting. These design "statements" screech "I'm special" and convince no one.

True individuality comes from honesty, not "creativity." It demands a clear appraisal of how you really live, of which things you truly value, of what mundane daily activities you especially enjoy. Cherish that creaky rocking chair? Keep it. Adore Scrabble? Make a place to play. Love to boogie? Give yourself room.

Expect that even in a genuinely individual residence, most household belongings will resemble your neighbor's. That's

REMEMBER, WHAT'S PERSONAL
IS MORE IMPORTANT THAN WHAT'S COOL.

because many of these common furnishings make sense. Couches are invaluable. Beds are sensible. As is a good food processor. Pity the family (mine) that decided that a rare seventeenth-century straw bench would be better than a plain old down sofa. Recognize instead that great design can still include IKEA lights and Pottery Barn chairs.

Furthermore, realize that even the most practical purchases can often be transformed from generic to personal by tailoring them to your needs. Turn a dull cabinet into a unique toy closet, for example, by adding bins, lowering the pulls to child height, and perhaps letting the kid paint the inside. Or morph that same box into a custom linen press with a few shelves, a couple of hooks, and maybe even a towel bar on the outside. Or give it wheels and a small hole in the back to make a one-of-a-kind mobile entertainment unit.

Problems arise, however, when everything comes from a single source, whether it be from a mail-order catalog or a trendy designer showroom. One-stop shopping may be an advertiser's dream, but who among us wants to be told what to covet and

In Burano, near Venice, houses are identified not by numbers but by the colors their owners paint them.

Opposite: Seashells transform a drab mantel into this spectacular centerpiece.

Overleaf: Interior of a tree house, Cotswold, England.

At the age of ten, this young English boy sold some of his toys to pay for this chandelier.

Opposite: To create a room that expresses who you are, you don't need a big budget—just a willingness to break some rules.

how to live? Your decor should come from your personality, not from a marketing department. Remember, what's personal is more important than what's cool. Having a great home should not involve keeping up with anybody. You *are* the Joneses.

Don't feel obliged to put yourself on display. More a Rorschach test than a diary entry, a personal home keeps some things secret. For example, any snapshots bearing your likeness between the ages of thirteen and seventeen should be squirreled away. Likewise, you may have loved your childhood dog, but thirty pictures of a dead poodle are more likely to contribute to

ITALIA
SYRIA
Il Trenino Giramondo

Some people like penthouses, others prefer treetops.

Opposite: Iconoclastic architect John Soane built rooms *around* his stuff—in this case, his collection of architectural details.

your isolation than to your decor. These personal details should probably be confined to your bedroom, if not your attic.

Most important, keep in mind that individuality is not the product of a decorative "touch" and it is not an afterthought. Identity comes from never forgetting who you are from beginning to end. Walt Whitman (not to mention Kool and the Gang) had the right idea: celebrate yourself. And your home will be great.

In the end, guidelines help but passion rules. If you can't live without grandpa's (cumbersome and creepy) stuffed moosehead collection, keep it. Similarly, once in a blue moon, a pink floor can be amazing. Just be sure you love it.

Swank couple, Los Angeles.

STYLE

GREAT DESIGN IS *SUPPOSED* TO BE BASED ON RATIONALITY. ITS BEAUTY, WE ARE TOLD, COMES FROM ITS LOGIC. ACCORDING TO THIS PERVASIVE SCHOOL OF THOUGHT, YOU SHOULD APPROACH CREATING A HOME LIKE ANY OTHER PROBLEM-SOLVING SITUATION. At least that's what architects claim. Decorators, in contrast, have always recognized the value of the personal and the quixotic, much to their disrepute. The design establishment tends to see decorators as flakes whose only role is to introduce new money to old furniture. "Pimps of taste [who] flourish in the red light district of culture," snarls critic Stephen Bayley.

Unfortunately, some are. With their hand-waving pronouncements ("Fabulous!"), these self-appointed tastemakers have perpetuated an equally suspect myth: that you need God-given talents in order to make a beautiful home.

STYLE IS WHAT SEPARATES THE SERVICEABLE FROM THE SUBLIME. AND IT DOESN'T HAVE TO MAKE PERFECT SENSE.

The truth lies somewhere in between: while a lot of design is based on solving problems, some of it is arbitrary. This is where style comes in. Style is what separates the serviceable from the sublime. And it doesn't have to make perfect sense.

Spectacular style is not reserved for the aesthetically gifted. On the contrary, "taste," the capacity to discriminate, is an ability we all share. Every client I have ever had has told me at one point "I know what I like, but . . ." "*But*" nothing. You know what you like. Period. Be confident.

Although style is important, remember that it's not, as Strunk and White rightly observe, a "garnish for the meat of prose." Rather, "Style has no such separate entity: it is non-detachable, unfilterable."

Good advice. To put it into action, bear the following in mind:

KEEP IT REAL Your home has to be true to its roots. That post-war condo is never going to look like an eighteenth-century farmhouse. Accept it or move. Under no circumstance try to make your living space into something it's not. It'll just end up looking fake.

Great style comes in many guises, from the pared down to the exuberant.

Overleaf: The designer of this room merged his Asian heritage with a modern sensibility, creating a room of tremendous style.

TO BE REALLY STYLISH, YOU NEED A TOUCH OF BAD TASTE.

Diana Vreeland's all-red apartment, Pierre Cardin's lunar villa—or this family's vinyl couch *(opposite)* may not be to everyone's taste but the message is universal: great design often requires taking some risks.

GO FOR TIMELESSNESS Temper the urge to dive whole hog into the latest decorating craze. Orange may be your new favorite color, but you're better off with a citrus flower arrangement rather than a Popsicle-colored living room. Indulge in trendiness on a smaller scale—and you'll never have to answer the question "What was I thinking?"

BEWARE OF "GOOD TASTE" Over the past decade, good taste has reached epidemic proportions. Everyone seems to have it. All you have to do is walk into a Gap. But sanitized and smoothed out, too much good taste can be numbing. Unless you are running for office and need to throw fund-raisers in your living room, do you really want a home whose chief virtue is that it offends no one? As the French say, it's better to have bad taste than very little.

In fact, real style involves a little bit of a risk. Former *Vogue* editor Diana Vreeland's apartment was ablaze in Chinese red. More recently, a designer made his name by draping his windows with cashmere curtains. Bill Blass, no slouch himself, advocates a decorative approach that is less expensive but just as off-kilter: buy a few easy chairs and some dogs to sit in them. Whatever your comfort level—and the limit may be a cashmere throw—allow your home to have at least one terrific aspect that raises an eyebrow.

DELTAPINE

Opposite: Keep in mind that everything need not match.

DISTRUST STYLE GIMMICKS To "add visual interest" and "get a food theme going," one designer has recommended dangling "long curly orange rinds from the exhaust hood over the stove." Please, leave them in the bowl. Style guru Chris Madden offers similarly dodgy "hints," such as using an old cowboy boot for flowers. But great style is the product of a full life, not a cheap gimmick. Even a florist's vase, the cheesy remnant of a remarkable date, is better than an old shoe.

RECOGNIZE THAT CONTEXT IS EVERYTHING The maharaja of Udaipur's jewel-encrusted palace looks great in Rajasthan. A shingle-style cottage sits perfectly on a Nantucket bluff. A Victorian brownstone is just right in Manhattan. Move them around and you are in trouble. What's beautiful in one place doesn't necessarily work in another. The same goes for almost every element of your home. Pink satin curtains shine in the maharaja's domain. In New York, they just make you look like a bad hairdresser.

TRADITION IS DIFFERENT FROM CONVENTION Respecting the past is different from mindlessly imitating it. So keep great-grandma's dining table; just don't try to reproduce her house.

EVERYTHING NEED NOT MATCH You may be the rare person who loves Gustav Stickley so much that you want every piece of

Great design does not begin with a truckload of trendy furniture. A zebra rug, a Saarinen chair, and a crystal trash can *(above)* say more about the residents' insecurity than their sense of style.

Opposite: True style never tries too hard. The most stylish rooms reveal who their owners are, not what magazines they read.

furniture in your home to be by his hand. That's fine. But most of us are naturally more eclectic. And this is good since great style often grows from contrast—a highly carved Indian chest in a sleek loft, a Corbusier chaise in a Federal-style town house. Curtains need not (better not) mimic upholstery. Aim instead for a home that is balanced but not hyper-coordinated. End tables should complement one another but need not be identical. Depending upon your sofa's position, you may not even need two at all. Ditto your bed. Nor do woods have to match. What you want to avoid is *almost* matching—grandma's Regency desk with the Bombay Company's "Regency" trash can. Like wearing gray socks in two different shades, the results will clash.

DON'T TRY TO BE COOL Unless trendiness is your life's mission, don't bother. It takes too much effort and too much money to keep changing things.

The key to style lies less in swatches than in substance. Hardly superficial, great style resolves the conundrum that's at the heart of all design: balancing the need for common-sense and long-range planning with the desire to express who we are at a given time. A truly stylish home is one that can keep up with you but never seems out of date. The balance can be tricky, but so is riding a bike.

Two friends at Stonehenge.

SIMPLICITY

DESPITE ITS 153 ROOMS, JAPAN'S IMPERIAL VILLA, KATSURA, IS AS SIMPLE AS THEY COME. CONSTRUCTED WITH TIMBER FRAMING, ALL SPACES ARE LAID OUT IN MULTIPLES OF THE TATAMI MATS. MATERIALS ARE LIMITED TO WOOD, STONE, AND STRAW, and even these have hardly been altered. Paths are made from river-smoothed rocks. Joints have no nails. Some wood still has the bark on it.

According to scholar John Norwich, Katsura is a palace that derives its aesthetic from mountain huts and farmers' cottages. The *sukiya* style, as it is called, emphasizes harmony founded on simplicity. The result is a house that is huge but intimate, restrained but relaxing.

PLAIN IS NOT SIMPLE

Although architect John Pawson's residence shares Katsura's minimal aesthetic, his London town house is anything but homey. This bland shell looks like a shoebox and has about as much character.

With thousands spent on hiding all signs of human habitation, this London kitchen is more boring than beautiful, whereas the gently colorful stair *(opposite)* is anything but dead.

The same Douglas fir used for the floorboards is used for the dining table and the bed. And don't even mention personal objects. Anything that interrupts the hollow perfection has been banished. Just try finding the toilet. It's a place where design with a capital *D* rules and the inhabitants, for which it is theoretically intended, have to make do, cleaning up as they go along and hiding any sign of human habitation; a place where restraint has been replaced by emptiness.

The galling irony is that this elitist poverty is only for the wealthy. Imagine how much it costs to hide all signs of human activity in those custom-made, invisible cabinets.

Unfortunately, Pawson is not the only domestic tyrant. Many designers are professional control freaks. Frank Lloyd Wright, while sensible in theory, could be dictatorial at home. He forbade his wife Catherine to wear anything but dun-colored clothes so as not to clash with their house's color scheme. She assented. And then he left her for a client's wife.

So what's the moral of the story? Chuck your furniture and run out for some tatami mats? Hardly. In truth, while no one

"FIVE LINES WHERE THREE IS ENOUGH IS ALWAYS STUPIDITY. NINE POUNDS WHERE THREE ARE SUFFICIENT IS OBESITY. BUT TO ELIMINATE EXPRESSIVE WORDS IN SPEAKING OR WRITING—WORDS THAT INTENSIFY OR VIVIFY MEANING—IS NOT SIMPLICITY, NOR IS SIMILAR ELIMINATION IN ARCHITECTURE SIMPLICITY. IT MAY BE, AND USUALLY IS, STUPIDITY."

— FRANK LLOYD WRIGHT

THE KEY IS TO UNDERSTAND THAT
SIMPLE DOESN'T IMPLY SPARTAN.

could be at ease in a Pawson box, few Westerners could live comfortably in a Japanese house. The key is to understand that simple doesn't imply spartan. Rather, it means have what you need in order to make your house a home. No less.

And no more. For many of us, the real temptation is to pile on the possessions, a desire as manic as Pawson's obsession to do without. Often we think that if we just had one more thing, our homes would be complete. Not true. Each room in your house does not have to be a different color; each window treatment does not need a unique fabric. If you find yourself adding stuff to make your home feel better, it's probably because you have forgotten to identify what's really important.

It's a temptation for which I have a lot of empathy. Designers tend to want to design, but once in a while just the opposite is required. Sometimes you've got to know what to leave alone. Part of simplicity has nothing to do with paring down, but with not doing too much.

When I moved into my old studio, I was raring to go. After all, this was going to be my headquarters, the physical incarna-

Decorated with colorful murals and pinned-up family photos, Le Corbusier's beach hideaway provides all the essentials for relaxed living: a lamp for reading, a window for watching the sunset, and just enough storage to hold a beach towel.

Opposite: Simple but luxurious, this white room sparkles with voluptuous materials, rich architectural detail, and lots of cushy pillows.

Truly simple interiors allow for everything necessary, but nothing more.

tion of a design philosophy, a reflection of my individual identity. Thankfully, my bank account lagged behind my ambition, giving me the time to realize that this place did not need much help. Located atop a former department store, the 4,500-square-foot penthouse loft was in good repair and featured 35-foot ceilings as well as a cast iron staircase leading to a tower room with 360-degree views and a rooftop terrace. The approach was clear: don't fix what ain't broke.

So keep your eye on the ball and, as Einstein put it, "Make things as simple as possible, but no simpler."

Mahatma Gandhi's home office, Bombay, India.

FLEXIBILITY

FEW OF US HAVE ROOMS FOR EVERY NEED. WE ENTERTAIN IN THE KITCHEN, EAT IN THE LIVING ROOM, AND WORK IN THE BEDROOM. PLAN FOR THIS RANGE OF ACTIVITY. DO YOU LIKE TO WATCH TV WHEN YOU EAT? Forget balancing plates on your knees. Give yourself a place to put them. If you do your best thinking in the bathroom, consider putting a small chair there.

But flexibility is not just for those us with limited space. Even castle dwellers need to respond to a fundamental human need: the desire to be both together and alone at the same time or, rather, to do separate things in the same room at the same time. How many living rooms, for instance, are underused because one member of a family can't read while the other is watching TV?

The solution is maximalism: to make within each room a series of places that can be used for various functions.

In truth, multifunctional homes have been around at least as long as the Middle Ages, when homes had very few private spaces.

CONTINUOUS PRIMPING, POOFING, FOLDING, UNFOLDING, STASHING, AND DRAGGING ARE SIGNS THAT YOU ARE WORKING TOO HARD TO BE COMFORTABLE.

The central room, the Great Hall, was the place to sit, eat, and sleep (often with several others in the same bed). Most of the furniture was foldable and stored at the sides of the rooms when not in use.

Sometimes flexibility can be built into the furniture itself. This picture frame *(above)* folds down *(opposite)* to make a breakfast table.

Contemporary homes are more private but need to be just as flexible. One client, a television-obsessed graphic designer, dreamed of a screen that she could "pull behind her" and watch from anywhere in her apartment. We fulfilled her fantasy by punching a hole in the wall between the living room and the bedroom and installing a TV on a revolving base, thereby allowing her to watch from any room at any angle. In case she ever tires of reruns, we also gave our client something else to look at by mounting a mirror on the back of this oiled cherry unit, which, coupled with the shelves below, doubles as a vanity.

Your most treasured companion may be your child rather than your TV, but with a little forethought, your living room should function just as well for both parents and kids. To make a place that is relaxing for adults and fun for children, keep in mind that the room has to address both generations' needs. Naturally floor-oriented, children need to be able to make messes, explore, hide. Adults, on the other hand, want to engage in sedentary activities within eyeshot of their kids. You can help reconcile these diametrically opposed activities by imagining a horizontal line running about two feet above the floor. Above is your do-

Juicy
Juicy
Fru-t
Fru-t
Extra Cheese
Sausage
Mushroom
Pepperoni
CUSTOMER
Onions
Anchovies
Special

Home Office

The home office is not a new idea. Long before we had offices, we worked where we lived. Think cottage industries.

Think also of Thomas Jefferson, whose study at Monticello is one of the best domestic work environments ever designed. Despite its small size, approximately 120 square feet, this eighteenth-century space includes almost everything you would expect in a twenty-first-century working environment: an ergonomic high-backed chair with ottoman footrest; built-in task lighting (candles) on the arms; a rotating book stand that holds four times as many pages as the Staples equivalent. The forward-thinking president even had a copier—a pantograph of his own design.

One unfortunate recent development is that the anytime-anywhere office has become the all the time–everywhere workplace. Oh well.

Just because you can work at home doesn't mean you should try to reproduce your office and then hide it in some hideous cabinet that screams "Don't look at me." A home office needs to be simple and efficient, flexible and warm, but no more. In short, it should be the place that allows you to work best. Mark Twain worked in bed. So did Winston Churchill. Mahatma Gandhi preferred the floor. You decide what's best for you (see Appendix B for how).

main; beneath rule the children. Similarly, you can assign certain areas of the room to certain activities, allowing you to share the room but not each other's exact location. (The adults can spread out in the central seating area and allow the kids to take over the window nook, for example.)

This adjustable coffee table can be raised to transform the living area into a dining room.

This same idea—zones of use—can solve a multitude of similar problems, most commonly with home offices. Ideally you'd have an extra room in which to set up a work space (see Appendix B for more detail on home offices), but if you don't, flexibility is the key. Whatever the scale, the principle remains the same: good homes accommodate their occupants, not the other way around.

Pork pie, Birmingham, Alabama.

OTHER SENSES

BURNISHED LEATHER. APPLE PIE. MILES DAVIS. WHILE DESIGN IS PRIMARILY A VISUAL MEDIUM, IT IS NOT EXCLUSIVELY SO. TO BE TRULY GREAT, A DESIGN HAS TO STIMULATE ALL OUR SENSES.

TOUCH

As one of the Seven Wonders of the World, the Taj Mahal offers a lot to admire: the walls encrusted with semiprecious stones, the minarets tilted outward to make up for the narrowing effects of perspective, the awesome dome.

But one of the most powerful design elements is underfoot: the alabaster paving smoothed by millions of barefoot visitors. Despite its grand scale, the Taj Mahal feels intimate because you experience it in your stocking feet, which is probably what its builder, Shah Jahan, had in mind. The Mogul leader erected the Taj to honor his wife, Mumtaz Mahal, whose death in childbirth in 1631 left Jahan so heartbroken that his hair is said to have turned gray overnight. Worse, upon its completion, the romantic emperor was thrown in a nearby jail by his more pragmatic son,

Good food and good homes are so inextricably tied that, occasionally, it is hard to distinguish where one stops and the other starts.

leaving the elderly widower to spend his last seventeen years looking out at his wife's tomb, just out of reach.

You may have neither the shah's resources nor, hopefully, his love life, but you should recognize that touch plays a role in even the most humble abode. For the rest of us, design gets personal the moment we touch the front door. As Stanley Abercrombie, former editor in chief of *Interior Design,* writes, "the doorknob is the home's handshake," the welcoming gesture, the first acquaintance. Sensitive to design's tactile qualities, Finnish architect Alvar Aalto wrapped leather around the door handles of his Villa Mairea. Noticing that we tend to sweep our hands across surfaces as we walk through spaces, he also sewed cowhide bands across the living room columns.

We all know what feels good: the softness of flannel, the smoothness of a river rock. To see what role touch can play in your home, keep track of what you handle over half an hour. What is pleasing? Anything (pardon the pun) rub you the wrong way? A sisal carpet may look terrific, for instance, but for someone who walks around shoeless, it can be murder on the feet. If you really want to find out how a room feels, ask a child. Kids naturally want to touch everything, to drag their hands along a wall, to pick up whatever's not nailed down. They intuitively know that touch supplies opportunities for pleasure as strong as anything we get just using our eyes.

SMELL

Close your eyes. Imagine a truffle risotto. Inhale.

Smells draw us together as powerfully as any furniture arrangement. Smell is subconscious, preconscious, damn powerful. Smell brings you in. It takes you back.

Mosques have sometimes been made with scented mortar. Churches have long been enlivened by frankincense and myrrh. At home, give aromas their due, but with one caveat. Try not to resort to the cynicism that motivates retailers with their hidden misters. Homes crammed with potpourri are about as desirable as men soaked in aftershave. Instead, let pleasant scents emerge from the daily activities of a well-loved house. Freshly washed sheets, spring breezes, and kitchen herbs exude aromas that are more subtle yet more powerful than any upscale air freshener. Pleasant smells, like the other elements of your design scheme, should arise naturally from a well-designed home, not applied like some decorative flourish. So light your oven instead of scented candles, which brings me to the next point.

TASTE

Spend months and millions on the dream home and you may end up with a perfect house that's perfectly lifeless. To animate it, you need to have food. Eating is communal. Eating is primal. It matters little if the meal is pizza and beer or bordeaux and rack of lamb: food brings us together. But if you ask me, risotto works the best.

The way things feel can be as important as the way they look—imagine the sensation of polished marble under bare feet at the Taj Mahal, or in your own bathroom.

Overleaf: As Freud recognized (his consulting room bulletin board is on the left), memory is an important part of a great interior.

Sound Advice

Not all sound is created alike. A bird song isn't a traffic jam.

To eliminate distracting noise, use common sense. Pick those areas that are naturally calmest for the quietest activities. Don't panic. Before you move in, empty houses often echo. Add the furniture and the problem often disappears as all those surfaces break up the sound waves. Rugs and curtains also help, but for the most stubborn problems, books are your strongest weapon. A couple dozen of these natural baffles dampen sound as effectively as a plaster wall. And you thought libraries were quiet because of the librarians.

When buying new items, keep sound in mind. Plan to leave the windows open a lot? Try billowing curtains instead of clanging venetian blinds. Want a quieter desk area? A large pinup board will help. Noisy neighbor? Try a nasty note.

HEARING

Anyone who's ever been stuck in an otherwise beautiful room with a screaming two-year-old knows the effect hearing can have on our experience of a place. Because most designers view sound as about as desirable as a hysterical toddler, they focus on getting rid of it. And, especially in cities, this aim makes sense.

But who wants to silence rustling leaves and warbling birds? Do you really want to dampen laughter? Isn't your home cozier during a thunderstorm? A more enlightened point of view eliminates not all sound, but all noise.

MEMORY

Great design stimulates more than the physical senses. Some of the most important elements in our homes draw strength from the associations they conjure rather than from the way they look. A Little League photo. A cherished LP. Your grandma's hutch.

To see is also to remember.

Occasionally, memory can inspire whole schemes. In his renovation of an 1820s New York town house, for instance, architect James Wines lightly plastered over the remnants of the original Greek Revival interior to create a series of "artifacts" that partially emerge from the walls. These "ghosted memories" include bookcases, mantelpieces, and even a table that pokes through the flat surface of the wall.

In this renovation of an early-nineteenth-century Greenwich Village townhouse, plaster "ghosts" recall the original owner's life.

In your space, associations may play a smaller but no less evocative role: a grouping of family photos or, as in my childhood home, a series of pencil marks on the wall documenting my growth.

At times, though, the past can overwhelm the present. A friend whose father was a prominent oilman covered his bathroom with framed corporate portraits of Dad's forty closest business associates, an intimidating collection, particularly when viewed from the toilet. But few people could outdo one college acquaintance, a young English lord so hell-bent on trumpeting his aristocratic roots that he dragged a seven-foot oil portrait of himself at eighteen, complete with the family crest, to his dorm room.

Most important, resist the temptation to lapse into nostalgia. Slavishly recreate the past and you'll end up with a personal theme park, a kind of domestic Disneyland. Go "period" and it will feel fake. To be unforgettable, memories have to come from something real: the building's history, or your own.

Ray and Charles Eames, Venice, California.

CONSTRAINTS

A CLOSETFUL OF CASH, A BOATLOAD OF WORKERS, AND A COUPLE OF YEARS WILL GET YOU AN EXPENSIVE, LABOR-INTENSIVE HOME THAT TAKES FOREVER TO COMPLETE. IT MIGHT BE GOOD. MORE OFTEN, HOWEVER, GREAT DESIGN COMES FROM HAVING IMPERFECT CIRCUMSTANCES, FROM HAVING TOO LITTLE MONEY, LABOR, AND TIME. Only then are you forced to figure out what's really important and invent better ways of achieving it.

During World War II, the U.S. Navy approached architect and furniture designer Charles Eames about making splints for wounded servicemen. Building upon some early trials with a homemade plywood-forming machine (nicknamed "Kazam!"), Eames set out to develop lightweight splints from one of the few readily available wartime materials. Out of these experiments, he perfected a system for molding plywood, which then inspired one of the most recognizable furniture designs of the twentieth

The Eameses knew how to work with limitations. A wartime dearth of good wood led them to develop one of the most recognizable designs of the twentieth century, the LCW (aka the Potato Chip Chair).

Opposite: Unusual spaces like this narrow loft can work better than their more everyday counterparts. This tight place, for instance, actually makes for a cozier dining area than a more spacious room.

century, the LCW, or, as it is more commonly known, the Potato Chip Chair. As Eames remarked, "Design depends largely on constraints."

At the other extreme, Hummer king Ira Rennert is building an overblown Viagra of a house next door to my Long Island shack. For their weekend getaway, Rennert and his wife have set aside sixty-three seaside acres to build the largest private home in America: 100,000 square feet, twenty-nine bedrooms (they have two children), thirty-six bathrooms, and a 200-car garage. With few budget restrictions, my students often make the same mistake by cramming their spaces with expensive knickknacks. The results are places where everything is important but nothing matters.

This solid gold toilet may seem excessive, but compare it to Versailles in the jungle, Mobutu Sese Seko's country house. The late Zairean dictator spent an estimated two billion dollars on this. A pink marble monolith complete with its own hydroelectric dam and international airport, the remote palace also features computer-operated fountains, flowers imported from South Africa, and five thousand Venezuelan long-hair sheep. Sadly, it never made the cover of *Architectural Digest.*

Opposite: An attic study is successful because of the peaked roof, not in spite of it.

Thankfully, most of us are not in the position to make such Olympic-size belly flops. For the rest of us, limitations make designing easier by eliminating choices (e.g., what to do with an extra million dollars). One friend's triangular living room, for instance, seemed daunting until she realized that it gave her the perfect place to read. Another's pal's loft was saddled with the plugged-up remains of an old elevator shaft—a burden until he realized that the columned nook is just big enough for a bed and works like a built-in canopy.

Good designers, whether they have ten years or ten days, ten million or ten dollars, know that successful homes focus on a few special elements executed with great authority: a spectacular fireplace, an amazing kilim, or, as we provided in a recent project, one striking photograph—mounted on the ceiling. In this way, making a home is not unlike writing: set the scene, tell a story, and give 'em a great climax.

A hearth floor from Jacques Tati's film *Mon Oncle*.

MISTAKES

WE ALL KNOW THE SCENARIO (EVEN THE PROFESSIONALS): YOU COME IN WITH BEST-LAID PLANS AND SOMEHOW IT GOES WRONG. TERRIBLY WRONG. WHAT LOOKED LIKE A SIMPLE TASK FOR A LAZY WEEKEND IS NOW YOUR WORST NIGHTMARE. RELAX. Sometimes you've got to mess up to move forward. I should know.

A couple of years ago, I had the bright idea to make pre-stained table linens. So I tried coffee rings. Spaghetti swirls. Wine spills. Jam prints. I kept searching for the perfect stain. Bad idea. After four months, I had a truckload of some of the ugliest, not to mention most expensive, place mats you've ever seen.

Still, my efforts weren't in vain. These screwups got me thinking about how and for what table linens are used. In so doing, I consulted Amy Vanderbilt's *Etiquette: A Guide to Gracious Living* and realized that I didn't really know what to do with my soup spoon and bread plate, not to mention my sherry glass and oyster fork.

"A DOCTOR CAN BURY HIS MISTAKES BUT
AN ARCHITECT CAN ONLY ADVISE HIS CLIENT TO PLANT VINES."
—FRANK LLOYD WRIGHT

A big screw-up led to one of my biggest breakthroughs, and now the Etiquette Table Linen series is part of the permanent collection of the Cooper-Hewitt, National Design Museum.

Opposite: A narrow hallway might seem to be the last place where you'd want to pull out the stops, but all that attention pays off in this dramatic corridor. Getting there is now half the fun.

Overleaf: Carl Larsson's inviting sitting room features two floor levels, the result of a hasty addition.

So I designed the Etiquette place mat series, which shows you where to put your stuff. Accompanying napkins show you how to fold them into a fan, chevron, or lily. They are now part of the permanent collection of the Cooper-Hewitt, National Design Museum.

I'm not the only one to make something of an error. Some of the world's greatest architectural monuments were in fact mistakes-turned-masterpieces.

Although the Empire State Building may be the world's most recognizable skyscraper, its iconic spire was originally intended not as an architectural statement but as a dirigible mooring post. A similar lack of intention also characterizes the leaning tower of Pisa, which would be a lot less memorable if it stood straight.

The Japanese go a step further, seeking excellence through imperfection. At the heart of their quest is the concept of *wabi-sabi,* which loosely translated means "worn simplicity." *Wabi-sabi* describes an aesthetic outlook that finds true beauty to be rooted in flaws. It values the impermanent and the incomplete, the modest and the humble, the unconventional.

You only need to see a snapshot to know that Sweden's most famous house, the home of painter Carl Larsson, isn't perfect. Over twenty years, the turn-of-the-century cottage was not so much built as cobbled together. The windows don't match;

neither does the paint; the stairs are crooked; the plan looks clumsy to even the most untutored amateur. But this remote hodgepodge is among the most visited landmarks in Scandinavia. And these screwups are the reason why.

The Larssons were constantly inventing new ways of using their space, transforming a leftover doorway into a cupboard or keeping an obsolete second-story window to allow for a bird's-eye peek into the artist's painting studio below. One effect of these ad hoc renovations was to create a large variety of spaces. Throughout the house, you find little raised sitting areas and concealed nooks; there are literally dozens of small places in which to read, paint, daydream, and snooze. All that ease makes the Larsson house live up to its sobriquet as the most comfortable house in Sweden.

Although Larsson and his family were relentlessly unafraid to experiment with their house, you can imagine that even Larsson was apprehensive when his wife wrote while he was on a trip that she had just painted the dining room (including the bookshelves, benches, and grandfather clock) bright red and green. Although not perfect, the effect is again to make the room come alive.

According to Frank Gehry, "All great architecture leaks." He was probably referring to the buildings of Frank Lloyd Wright. For all his architectural genius, the most innovative twentieth-century architect couldn't keep the water out of his houses. They don't call this one "Fallingwater" for nothing.

You need not be so committed to improvisation, but you should remain loose. The trick is to make the right kind of mistakes. Undesirable errors are just that: money-wasting, cringe-making, and usually avoidable foul-ups. But take heart; prevention is easy. To avoid these decorative blunders, do the following:

THINK AHEAD Don't order that dream sofa, for example, before you measure your door openings.

REMEMBER THE BIG PICTURE Don't get fixated on something small (e.g., the color of your throw pillows) at the expense of the larger issues (a really comfortable place on which to throw them).

An all-blue room is celestial heaven for some, indigo hell for others; before you make a move like this, know how much risk you're comfortable with.

BE REALISTIC It's tempting to underestimate the effort involved in making an ideal living place. Don't fall into this trap. If you've done a good job, it will probably cost 10 to 15 percent more than you budgeted and take about 50 percent more time.

BE PRUDENT Aim for risks akin to crossing a street rather than jumping out of an airplane. If you're not sure about a chair, fifty bucks is a decent risk, but walk away if it's $5,000. Master your own screw driving but avoid welding.

To allow for fortuitous screwups, create a budget, plan ahead, then experiment. Short of doing your own roofing, the biggest mistake you're likely to make is with color. And even that is hardly tragic. So your walls are the wrong shade—big deal. Not only can you repaint, but another light coat of a contrasting color can even enrich the surface. Spilled some? Relax. You may even want to add more (the Swedes often painted "rugs" on their wood floors). The point is: if it doesn't turn out the way you expected, don't beat yourself up. That apparent disaster is almost always fixable and occasionally may even be a blessing in disguise.

START HERE

HOW TO MAKE A HOUSE A HOME

ASKING QUESTIONS

Simplicity, flexibility, style, and individualism—with these themes in mind, start making it happen. Regardless of size, budget, or time, every design goes through the same stages, the first—and most important—of which involves self-interrogation.

WHAT DO YOU HAVE?

Before you go whipping out credit cards and hefting paint cans, the first step in any design project is to figure out what you've got. Designers call this "defining the problem" (or, more euphemistically, the "challenge"). Start with your stuff. Make a list. By freeing your possessions from their context (e.g., that pile in the corner), it will be easier to imagine moving them around. Remember to count the things that are not home furnishings but nonetheless take up space, like bikes as well as books, magazines, CDs, and videos. Take inventory. Don't waste time, however, counting every volume—just measure how many linear feet you've got (this will help in planning). For example, a three-foot-wide bookcase with five shelves holds fifteen feet of books. Likewise, don't tally every shred of paper; just note that you have two drawers' worth.

Scrutinize what remains (it helps, if possible, to put all of it in one area). Is there some way of categorizing the miscellaneous items? This is where clutter lurks, so look hard. You may discover, like me, that you have fourteen umbrellas. Or thirty-seven bottles of moisturizer.

A living space is more than the sum of its objects. To get a clear picture of what you've got, you also need to evaluate how it all comes together.

WHAT WORKS?

What do you like best about your home? If the living room has technicolor sunsets, plan for an activity that lets you enjoy them. To enjoy its early evening prime, maybe this area should really be the place for dinner. If the northern views are endless with not a person in sight, do the windows really need "treatments"? Let common sense be your guide.

Where do you spend the most time in your house? When? What makes it so inviting? What do you do there—drink coffee and read the paper or snooze? If you are gone from morning until late, then the bedroom may be the place in which you spend the most time. Make it a high priority in terms of effort and expense. Superfancy sheets here, for example, may be more worthwhile than superfancy upholstery fabric in a rarely used sitting area.

What would you grab if your house were burning down?

Are there objects you love? A comfy chair or an old photo? Put these treasured things in places where you will use and see them.

What are your home's most outstanding architectural features? If you've got high ceilings, draw attention to them with an unusual color. Parquet floors? Resist the urge to carpet. Really big closets? Rejoice.

WHAT DOESN'T WORK?

What would you change about your home or about the way you live in it? Do you tend to accumulate piles? If so, of what? Books? Underwear? Where? If you have magazines everywhere, make a place to put them. Or lose them.

What are you afraid guests will see? Your home's most embarrassing elements are a good place to start fixing. Bathrooms are often disasters. They demand surgical hygiene but are packed with too much junk to make that possible. Extra shelves will often help. So will a ruthless edit of shampoo bottles.

Where do you eat? If you like to plop in front of the TV, get a really nice tray. Better yet, how about a small folding table that allows you to eat in style? More important (and common), if the dining room is underused, give new life to this dinosaur by providing for another activity. Maybe this

Sunday-night-supper relic is also a home office.

Do you work from home? If you do so often, then make a real place, as comfortable as home but as efficient as an office. Provide enough privacy, plenty of storage, and if you expect visitors, places for them to sit. Do you work at home only occasionally? Forgo the extra seating but keep the rest. Rarely? A fold-down surface may be all you need.

Are you a slob? Instead of hoping you will reform, arrange your home with a realistic self-portrait in mind. Let mail pile up, for instance? Make sure that you provide a covered place to put it.

WHAT DO YOU WANT?

The fun part comes when you get to ask what you wish you had. A guest bedroom? A library? A place to play boccie? Do you dream of Morocco? Soho? The warmth of grandma's house in Topeka?

In answering these questions, be honest about what you really like and dislike. Consult family members/spouses/life partners. What do they want? To get a better idea of who really wants what, make separate lists and then discuss. The goal is to figure out what's really important. To design is to see possibilities.

Eighty-eight pairs of underwear, Darjeeling, India.

ELIMINATING CLUTTER

NOW THAT YOU'VE SET PRIORITIES, PUT THEM INTO ACTION. THE CHALLENGE IS TO TRANSLATE A WISH LIST INTO A DREAM HOUSE. START BY GETTING RID OF THE DROSS.

Throwing it out

You want to make your home better, so the first thing you ask is: What can I buy? Wrong. For most of us, the problem isn't having enough; it's having too much (of the wrong stuff). Here's how to tell what should stay and what should go:

- If it's broken, fix it (this weekend) or forget it.
- If you can't remove the stains, remove what the stains are staining.
- If it's made of newsprint, get rid of it.
- If your ex gave it to you, throw it out.
- If your mother-in-law gave it to you, chances are you should throw it out.
- If the IRS sent it to you, keep it for at least seven years.

Too many expensive possessions are just as bad as too much crummy crap.

- If you don't plan to use it today, put it away. If you don't plan to use it within three months, store it. If you can't say, purge it.
- If the best thing about it is that it was cheap, toss it.
- If it's got "potential," actualize it (this weekend) or eliminate it.

Keep in mind that clutter-free does not mean compulsive; you want to organize your life, not hide all signs of it.

The amount of stuff will vary from household to household and from person to person. Come to a consensus, then organize what remains.

Where to put the rest

Like it or not, you've got stuff. And your home has to have places to put it. Use 20 percent of your total living space as a rough guideline for storage. Shocked? Well, just take a look at the bikes and computer boxes, not to mention suitcases and old files lining your halls and entries.

Storage is more than a necessary evil. It also presents a great design opportunity. While providing a home for your possessions, storage can effectively display a collection, define a seating area, or flesh out an awkward niche. At the same time, it can also look plain beautiful.

One more reason to unload: According to Dante, people who hold on to too much stuff go to the fourth circle of Upper Hell.

Overleaf: What you're storing can be prettier left out in the open than covered up.

FIGURE OUT WHAT YOU'RE STORING

Make a list divided into three categories: objects that are used daily, infrequently, and almost never. "Absolutely never" has, of course, already been chucked. The rest is simple: keep the things you need most nearest at hand, make the infrequent objects accessible, and stow the rest.

Be aware that certain mundane objects (e.g., wallets, keys) routinely come and go. Provide spots for these items, preferably at waist height where they're hard to lose—eye level, if you have small children—or you will find yourself cursing a lot.

INTEGRATE RATHER THAN SEGREGATE

Don't be ashamed of your possessions. Do you like stacks of magazines? Great. Instead of trying to stash them in the back of some overstuffed closet or oversize armoire, make them easy to

Registered
SAT-ISABGOL
FLEASEED HUSK!
THE SIDHPUR
SAT-ISABGOL FACTORY
FACTORY
QUAIL EGGS
IN WATER
NET WT. 15 OZ. (425g)
DRAINED WT. 8 OZ. (225g)
Camellia
RED KIDNEYS
Roland
BABY
Zatarain's
ROOT
BEER
EXTRACT
MAKERS OF
ROOT BEER
FOR 80 YEARS
3 FL. OZ.
SUNLIGHT
SOAP
ALASKA
condensed milk
leche condensada
WEL-PA
SQUID
PALO VIE
SUPER
BERMUDEZ & C.
EMPIRE
VIRGINIA
symphonia
Birinci
Kansas
PARISIENNES
POISON
PILLS
No. 983
BLAUD AND
STRYCHNINE
COMPOUND
LOTTE
CANDY
BLACK
KILLTOÏDS
FREE ZONE
COMMANDANTE
COMMANDING
GOTAS
AMOR
PERFUME

新亞薑糖
TING TING JAHE
GINGER CANDY
PRIDE
flour
all purpose
enriched • bleached
NET WT. 5 LBS. 2.26 kg.
CAFÉ
BUSTELO
SNACKTIME
PEANUTS
POCARI SWEAT
POWDER
WOOD DUNN
DAIRY MAID
CREAMERY BUTTER
Royal Top
БЕЛОМОРКАНАЛ
MaryLong
IDEALES
ARSENIC TRIOXIDE
ΕΛΜΑ
Belmont
Mt.d'or
RAILROAD MILLS
SWEET SCOTCH SNUFF
W.E. GARRETT & SONS
SWEET
LOTTE
Blue Berry
TIME

Hemingway's stash stood within easy reach of his study *(directly above)*. Maybe that's not everyone's priority, but the message is clear: Keep essentials close at hand.

Opposite: Why do the smallest apartments always end up with the biggest armoires? Opt instead for smaller pieces and greater variety—they work better and they look better.

find. In addition to making your house work better, displaying these items can work to improve its appearance. From piles of magazines to cans of coffee, many of the things we store are standardized and happen to look good grouped. Open storage will also add to your home's individuality by revealing your interests. And simple shelving is very inexpensive.

ACCESS IS MORE IMPORTANT THAN QUANTITY

Closets galore won't help if you can't reach or can't see what you're trying to find. A good rule of thumb is to store objects one-deep in appropriately sized cabinets. Two feet is ideal for blankets; two inches is perfect for Q-Tips.

CONSIDER BUILT-IN UNITS

Why do the tiniest apartments always seem to end up with the biggest armoires? Crammed with cherished photos, valuable stereo equipment, and even books, these tall and often flimsy pieces almost never work. Low ceilings just look lower. Floor space is smaller. And they never solve all your storage problems.

THE BOOK
of
KNOWLEDGE
Happy

What to Look For in a New Home

Making a home you love is easier if you start with something that has potential. Here's what to keep in mind:

LIGHT IS MORE IMPORTANT THAN YOU THOUGHT

Nothing affects a room as much as sunshine. But bright is not enough. More than quantity, your home needs sun in the right places at the right times. Look for rooms that get light when you are in them: a breakfast nook or bathroom that's sunny in the morning, a porch or living room that gets evening light.

WORRY MORE ABOUT LAYOUT THAN SIZE

A friend's 400-square-foot studio, for instance, feels anything but cramped. Unlike most shoebox single-room apartments, this one has a foyer with closet, a separate kitchen, a windowed hall with a terrace on the left, a pair of closets on the right, and a spacious bathroom at the end. Look for homes with a similarly varied layout. In particular, keep an eye out for spaces with good flow. Public areas like the kitchen should be near the front; private places like the bedroom should be further back; and in the middle, short corridors can join the two.

PLANNED STORAGE SHOULD TAKE UP 20 PERCENT OF YOUR LIVING SPACE

If the new place doesn't come with it, know that you'll need to add it somewhere.

Freestanding pieces would seem to be cheaper than custom-made cabinetry, and for the most part they are. Companies such as IKEA have armoires for as little as a hundred dollars. But to work best, these inexpensive cabinets often need to be customized, albeit without much trouble. In contrast, simple built-in shelves can be very reasonable and, since they are built to your specifications, very efficient.

Sometimes storage isn't just a necessity, it's a boon. With pieces that conceal, flip up, rotate, and display, this room looks as good as it works.

Overleaf: The storage in Frida Kahlo's home is as vibrant as her paintings.

SAVE SOME ROOM FOR SECRETS

Some storage deserves to be closed. It may only be a drawer, but we all need a place for our most intimate objects. Although small, this precious place allows you to reveal, to the right person, your first report card, the last letter your grandfather wrote, or that unfortunate snapshot taken the day you got your braces.

In this room the display of the computers is as carefully considered as the arrangement of the art or the furnishings.

Coping with your computer

We spend more on electronics than on anything else in our homes. And it shows. Technology often dominates our living spaces. Unfortunately, it's one area that design books tend to gloss over. But how can we ignore the six-foot tangle of wires that seems to sit in the middle of all our living rooms?

The secret? Put it in perspective. Think of it as a telephone. The computer is just the latest in a stream of technological developments (electricity, running water, central heating) and just as significant. But no more. Let's face it: you wouldn't design your house around your phone jacks. Your home should incorporate technology; it shouldn't be *about* it.

Covering it up can work, but only if the cover is a lot better than what it hides. A huge, cruddy armoire makes a big problem bigger. Don't make your thirty-two-inch TV the focal point of a room and then pretend we won't notice it behind those cabinet doors. Likewise, a speaker with a plant on top doesn't mask the speaker; it draws attention to it.

If you aren't going to hide the stuff, concentrate on shrinking the pile and, most important, making it more organized.

DOUBLE CHECK THAT YOU'VE THROWN OUT WHAT YOU CAN

Ask again, do I really need all this stuff? Now that the seventies have come and gone twice already, must I hang on to those KC and the Sunshine Band party tapes? Do I have to have the comprehensive Chicago LP collection? Can I make do for a couple of hours a night with just a laptop instead of a monster display?

DON'T BUY MORE THAN YOU NEED IN THE FIRST PLACE

Are you sure you gotta have the mouse and the joystick, the writing tablet and the microphone? How many times have you used that bread maker? Do you need a toaster if you're never home for breakfast?

Natural Selection

On a spring morning in 1575, Sen no Rikyu, the revered master of the Japanese tea ceremony, was expecting company. The powerful warlord, Toyotomi Hideyoshi, had come to see Rikyu's garden of morning glories, but when he arrived not a flower was in sight. Only after entering Rikyu's teahouse did Hideyoshi see a single beautiful morning glory displayed in the alcove. Rikyu, it turns out, had cut down all the other flowers to better focus attention on one single blossom.

TO BE SMART WITH MONEY AND GENTLE ON THE EARTH ARE NOT SPECIAL HATS BUT INTEGRAL PARTS OF EVERYDAY DESIGN.

REDUCE THE BULK

Look at what can be hung under the table top (not on the floor, where it gathers dust). In most cases, you should be able to fit the CPU and keyboard under the work surface. Try to orient the machine's back toward a wall. Confronting the rear end of your computer every time you walk into your living room is about as appealing as running into the business side of a pug.

ENTERTAINMENT CENTER, SHMENTERTAINMENT CENTER

There is no rule that all electronics have to be in the same place. To make them less monolithic, do the opposite of making a collection: consider separating the pieces. Put the stereo in one cabinet, the TV in another.

TAME THE CORDS

The real mess comes from the wires. Just unplugging and neatly replugging will alleviate 90 percent of the problem. Go a step further and bundle them (with rubber bands, if nothing else).

PLAN FOR THE JUNK

While making room for the machines, don't forget to allow shelves, drawers, and cabinets for the accompanying CDs, DVDs, and videos as well as for the attendant paper, software, and manuals.

Getting more — buy sparingly

A half-dozen well-chosen pieces is all most living rooms need.

The emphasis here is on doing the most with what you've got. Part of this rationale is economic: you should not have to start over in order to make a significant impact on your home. Part is environmental: Why consume when you can reuse? All of it has to do with good design. To be smart with money and gentle on the earth are not special hats but integral parts of everyday design. Still, there are times when you need or want more.

A couch is the single most important purchase for any home. It is essential gathering furniture, the fundamental piece around which one builds a seating arrangement. But buying one can be intimidating since it seems to require making a lot of decisions, not to mention spending a lot of money. It doesn't have to (for

If you're going to splurge, a sofa is a good place to do it, but spend the money on a piece that's well constructed.

help, see Appendix A,"A Really Good Sofa"). Other essentials include a pair of chairs, an adjustable light, an all-purpose table, and, of course, a bed. What these elements look like and how much they cost is up to you, but the criteria to evaluate these acquisitions should remain the same: Does this prospective purchase really solve a problem you've identified? Of course, every once in a while a new object will have no other purpose than to delight you. That's okay, too.

The obvious sources (Pottery Barn, etc.) can be good places to look for these staple elements. But to insure that your home expresses your individuality, limit yourself to one major purchase from a home furnishings chain. For something you will really love, check out nonstandard sources like garage sales, estate sales, antique shops, auctions, Salvation Army, and eBay, the online flea market. If you're feeling driven, make a pilgrimage to the mother of all fleas, the 3,000-dealer Brimfield Antiques Fair (see Resources).

But remember that not everything needs to be amazing. Great homes are the products of a few strong elements, not dozens of pieces clamouring for attention. Even if you had all the time and money in the world, it wouldn't be desirable to fill your house with one-of-a-kind dazzlers. So focus on a few things you really love. If you've got a gorgeous Jacobsen sofa, don't worry so much about a plain coffee table—you may not even need one.

That Flea Market Find

We've all heard the stories: a priceless armoire bought for a song. But where do you find this stuff? How can you tell if it's right for you? And once you get it home, how do you adapt that great-looking old cupboard to hold the stuff you need (like a VCR)?

The first rule of flea marketing is: be prepared. That means:

KNOW WHAT YOU WANT. With all that stuff around, you can get overwhelmed if you don't have a clear idea of what you need.

BE OPEN TO SURPRISE. While looking for that dining table you may find a great set of napkins.

GO EARLY. The best stuff goes fast.

PRAY FOR BAD WEATHER. Crummy conditions make for great bargains. You will find that cold, wet vendors are very flexible.

DRESS TO UN-IMPRESS. Your clothes should be loose and comfortable. They should make you look flinty, not chic.

BRING A BAG. I prefer knapsacks which leave my hands free. At larger markets, the ambitious bring carts.

TAKE A TAPE MEASURE. That nifty armoire may look great, but if it doesn't hold your TV, you're out of luck. Make sure any piece you covet will fit through the smallest place through which you must drag it (the front door, elevator, or door jamb). Check to see that it will hold what it needs to. Televisions require twenty-two inches; small stereos about a foot. Save yourself the schlepp by sizing up before you cart off.

BRUSH UP ON YOUR NEGOTIATING SKILLS. Practice disinterest, walking away, and cheerful-but-firm bargaining. Or just take along a hard-ass friend.

DON'T FORGET THE MONEY. Keep the wad hidden and your wallet filled just with what you think you'll need. For easier bargaining, bring many bills in small denominations.

Bulldog, London.

ARRANGING FURNITURE

CHANCES ARE, WHEN YOU FIRST SAW YOUR HOME, THE REAL ESTATE AGENT TOOK YOU AROUND TO EACH ROOM AND NAMED THEM: "NOW HERE'S THE FORMAL DINING ROOM, HERE'S THE SUN ROOM..." THE SUN ROOM? JUST BECAUSE YOUR ROOMS HAVE NAMES DOESN'T MEAN YOU HAVE TO USE THEM THAT WAY. A solarium might be a great place to work and have lunch and occasionally even tan. If you don't entertain often, a formal dining room might make more sense as a study, den, or office. Likewise, to see a bedroom merely as a mattress container is a crummy use of space. For most of us, the "bedroom" is no longer just a sleeping area but one that allows for a number of retreat-oriented activities—dressing, reading, and watching TV, as well as sleeping. So think of it that way. Instead of focusing on rooms, concentrate on places.

TO DESIGN IS TO PLAY, TO TRY THINGS OUT, TO TAKE RISKS.

As a rule, cluster gathering areas, the most public functions, near the entrance, and confine retreats, the more intimate spaces, to more naturally secluded areas. Along the way, mark the progression from public to private with a series of small spots to pause, relax, and talk. In creating both communal and private places, keep the following in mind:

The way the sun moves through rooms gives us clues as to how to use them best.

FIND THE HEART In older homes, the hearth was the heart: the place where meals were prepared and feet were warmed, a core more hypnotic than QVC. Your home may not have such an obvious center, but to be really alive, it needs a heart. Pick a natural convergence point—in theory the living room but, more probably, the kitchen, the bedroom (especially for those of us who work long hours), or wherever the TV is. Then orient subsidiary spaces around it.

LOOK AT THE SUN In choosing the varied identities of different spaces, look at the sun. Natural light is one of the most compelling elements of any design and your scheme should work with it. This means that if the so-called living room gets great sunsets, maybe it should really be the place you have dinner so you get to enjoy it (for more on this subject, see the "Using Light and Color" section, p. 135).

DON'T OVERLOOK HALLS AND STAIRS More than just ways to get from one space to another, halls and stairs can be places in

Look beyond your front door. Potential living space often lies just outside it.

Opposite: In-between places, like halls and stairs, can be as great as the rooms they link.

themselves and deserve as much thought as the rest of the house, especially if they are the first places to be seen. Make halls welcoming. Provide places for mail, gloves, or even a chair that lets you take off your shoes.

LOOK OUTSIDE Little spaces, such as a foyer, porch, or a few feet of ground out back, are worthy of as much consideration as your rooms. A spot under a tree or a place to put a table and two chairs can become extensions of your living area.

139·140·141·142

How to arrange furniture

Like a writer's outline, the furniture arrangement blocks out the major points of a room's design. It specifies what should take place where—knitting here, carousing there. As with writing, the only unforgivable error is not to decide what's important. At home, the symptom is sticking furniture along a room's edges in the misguided belief that such an arrangement will provide the most space. On the contrary, line up your cabinets like so many ex-cons, and your home will feel like a prison. Instead, jump in. To design is to play, to try things out, to take risks. Use the following guidelines as an excuse to experiment. Live with it for a

Furniture is well placed when it brings people together, not necessarily when it all lines up. Think bonfire, not airport lounge.

Opposite: Put furniture in the middle of the space where you use it rather than hiding it along its perimeter. The room will work better and will seem bigger than it would with everything stacked up along its edges.

Screens and shelves can divide space as well as walls.

couple of days. If you don't like it, move it. (Just make sure you put a towel under the heavy pieces.)

LISTEN TO YOUR ROOMS

Houses are almost always designed with a furniture layout in mind. Take a moment to survey the space. Look for clues. Many bedrooms are made with one wall that seems to be precisely a bed's width. Living areas are often conceived with ideal seating arrangements grouped around the principle focus, leaving room for people to pass without bumping into the furniture. Light fixtures can also give hints as to what to place below them. Two sconces on one wall probably flanked a significant piece of furniture. A hanging lamp in the dining room is a pretty good indicator of where the table's center was envisioned.

At the same time, recognize that some layouts are better than others. Just because the dining table was meant to be in the corner doesn't mean it needs to stay there. But it's a good place to start.

This is a classic seating circle in a distinctly modern room.

FIND A FOCUS

Just as every house has one heart, every room has its strongest feature. It may be a fireplace, a view, or even a favorite photo. Ask yourself, "What is the most important element?" and then build your seating arrangement around it.

MAKE A SITTING CIRCLE

Well-placed furniture brings people together. Start with the largest pieces, like the sofa. Cluster additional chairs in a well-defined area with paths running past, not cutting through, the grouping. Leave eighteen inches between a sofa and a coffee table and three feet for any place you want to walk. Add a few too many chairs (not too perfect). If you have room, create secondary seating arrangements. This may just mean a comfy chair by a window. The goal is to give you and your guests many different places to sit.

Keep the grouping balanced but not rigidly symmetrical. Gather *around* like a bonfire rather than *across* like a job interview. Likewise, choose similar but not necessarily identical chairs. Pay

THE MOVEMENT THROUGH ROOMS IS AS IMPORTANT AS THE ROOMS THEMSELVES.

The best dining rooms feel intimate because they are more cramped than you would think.

attention also to the scale of the pieces. We all want big cushy couches to settle into. But big is relative. A nine-foot sofa in a twelve-foot room is pretty much a disaster. Comfort comes from the seating's arrangement, not from its size.

You spend as much time walking around your living space as sitting in one spot, so make it easy to navigate. Avoid furniture obstacle courses that force you to cut around armoires and past couches to follow your daily routines. Remember: the movement through rooms is as important as the rooms themselves.

AIM FOR A PERFECT DINING ROOM

Like a great place to sit, a great place to eat fosters intimacy. Consequently, more important than the chairs, even the room, is the table. In Italy's Garfagnana area, furniture and food are actually united. The traditional meal in this secluded mountain region is polenta spread over a dining surface with a hole in the middle to hold sausages. Diners start at the table's edge and work inward, finally earning the right to devour the meat.

In your home, thirty-six inches wide allows enough room for the plates and glasses but still keeps you close. Narrower (but no less than thirty inches) can be even better. Just make sure you have plenty of places near the table on which to put platters, dishes, and extra wine. Tight spacing between chairs also helps. Allow eighteen inches of table length for each person. To keep

Madames

SO DON'T RELY ON YOUR FURNITURE PLACEMENT FOR ENLIGHTENMENT. AIM FOR CONTENTMENT INSTEAD.

people near enough to really see each other, do not allow for much more. And to bring them even closer, keep the centerpieces low and make a pool of light in the middle.

Created a century apart, both these rooms feature spaces made without using traditional walls. Carl Larsson concocted a room inside a room *(above)* by placing this canopied bed right in the middle of the floor. The modern space *(opposite)* uses open-backed shelving to divide the dining area from the living room.

DEFINE SPACE WITHOUT WALLS

We all want homes that are open and cozy. Much of this can be accomplished without resorting to major construction. The key is to play with the stuff you've got. Reinforce the major sitting areas with lighting or rugs. Be sensitive to the big impact small height changes can have. Seated at a dining table, for example, we can easily see over a two-foot-high piece of furniture and remain connected to the surrounding spaces. On the other hand, a three-foot-high piece, like a sideboard, defines a perimeter so that even in a large room, the dining *table* will now become the dining *area.* Use a screen or a bookcase to raise the edge another two feet, to slightly more than half the height of the average ceiling, and we will no longer be able to see beyond where we are sitting. The dining *area* will become a dining *room* within a room.

This strategy is especially effective in creating small retreats inside larger rooms. For instance, a single chair, no matter how well padded, can look lonely in a big space. To make it more inviting, pair that armchair with an adjustable lamp, a side table, and perhaps even a small rug. Nestle this grouping by a window and, presto, you've got a place to get away.

Goethe was as sensitive to his surroundings as he was to words. "Architecture," the renowned German poet once wrote, "is frozen music." Like the poet's own boudoir *(above)* the best bedrooms distance themselves from the surrounding spaces and allow us to retreat.

CREATE A RESTFUL BEDROOM

To make a bedroom feel more like a retreat, avoid placing the bed directly in your line of sight as you enter. Many bedrooms are designed for this major piece of furniture to lie against the entrance wall. With the head of the bed against the back of the room, the sleeper faces away from the house. Some experts, notably respected theorist Christopher Alexander, go even further and recommend that we sleep facing east. In order to avoid interrupting our REM sleep and to insure a good morning mood, he avers, we need to be awakened by the rising sun.

BEWARE OF *FENG SHUI*

Listening to your rooms should not be confused with *feng shui,* the Chinese art of placement. Not for dilettantes, *feng shui* is fine if you're an old Chinese guy or a serious scholar. Too often, however, it seems to be favored by the same people who seek spiritual enlightenment through aromatherapy and Yanni CDs. Besides, ever noticed how ugly *feng shui*–guided rooms are?

So don't rely on your furniture placement for enlightenment. Aim for contentment instead.

Union Station, Chicago.

USING LIGHT AND COLOR

IF THE FURNITURE ARRANGEMENT SETS THE STAGE, THE LIGHTING MAKES THE ACTION. ONE OF THE MOST POWERFUL ELEMENTS OF ANY GREAT DESIGN, THE RIGHT LIGHT ENCOURAGES ACTIVITIES TO TAKE PLACE WHERE THE FURNITURE SAYS IT SHOULD, whether it's eating or sleeping, paying bills or playing Scrabble, watching TV or just each other.

The right light also determines how things feel. It can relax, invigorate, or just decorate. For these reasons, lighting needs to be tackled early (even before color). Look at light the way you would at any other element of your scheme. To go about it, start by—you guessed it—asking more questions.

When do you use a particular room? In the morning with coffee? On a weekend afternoon while snoozing? Note that some rooms may look best when you are not there. With daylight streaming in through the windows, for instance, the living room may seem dreamy in the morning as you leave for work.

**THE RIGHT LIGHT ALSO DETERMINES HOW THINGS FEEL.
IT CAN RELAX, INVIGORATE, OR JUST DECORATE.**

The best light is sunlight, even in a bedroom. A rising sun ensures a better night's sleep by waking you naturally from the REM state.

Come back twelve hours later and a single bare bulb is grim. Don't fret. Just plan for it.

What do you do in each room? What do you *want* to do in each room? Ambient light may be fine for talking, but too bright for dining. A living room for entertaining a mother-in-law should be lit differently from one in which to make out (I'll let you decide which is darker). Specific activities, like reading or stamp collecting, require direct illumination (lamps). Think about where you sit and have sunshine or a light close by.

How do you want your rooms to feel? Cool like a Vermeer? Consider halogens or, better yet, a northern exposure. Steamy like a Gauguin? Try incandescent (i.e., regular) bulbs or a southern orientation.

To turn this wish list into reality, you have to be aware of some fundamental ideas:

SUNLIGHT IS BEST Cheap and plentiful, sunshine affects a room like nothing else. But bright is not enough. More than quantity, your home needs sun in the right places at the right times: a breakfast nook and bathroom that are cheery in the morning, a porch or living room that gets evening sun. Be sensitive to this orientation. Northern light, for example, is cooler, darker, and more even than its southern counterpart. Ideal for artists' studios, it can be dreary for living rooms. On the other

The Nitty-Gritty

Light is energy given off in the form of photons. This energy can be emitted from a number of sources:

NATURAL LIGHT is given off from the tumult on the sun's surface. Natural light is a designer's first choice. Use it when you can.

INCANDESCENT LIGHT, as in regular light bulbs, is the most familiar source. Although they are easy to find and cheap, the catch is that they are relatively expensive to run. That's why you do not find them in office buildings. On a small scale, however, incandescent light's warmth is well worth the added maintenance cost.

HALOGEN LAMPS are smaller and give off a brighter, whiter light that is more true to the sun than their incandescent cousins. The disadvantages are that halogens burn very hot and consume more electricity. Low-voltage halogens, the most common type of track lighting fixtures, require transformers, which can hum. Occasionally, although this is often due to mishandling, halogens have been known to explode.

FLUORESCENTS have a bad reputation. The older-style tubes, with their sterile greenish light, can make Christy Turlington look sickly. Moreover, they vibrate at 70,000 times a second, just slow enough for your brain to register the fluctuation. This is why sitting under fluorescents can make you feel sick. Newer "full spectrum" versions give off a more natural light. And they are very economical to run.

hand, southern light is brighter, warmer, and more varied and is perfect for heavily used rooms. But sunlight doesn't have to light your home to be pleasant. Just the sight of rays falling on a bench or filtering through the trees is a big plus.

ONE LIGHT SOURCE IS NOT ENOUGH A single bulb, no matter how bright, will create strong shadows. A hanging fixture may be perfect for a hall, for example, but brutal for a bedroom because of the shadows it casts. Additional light sources help build a balanced lighting pattern. Aim for more lights that are less bright, for more light sources rather than more wattage.

The most flattering artificial light comes from using a variety of low-placed lamps with gentle wattage.

BRIGHT IS BLAND Blast a big enough halogen at the ceiling and you'll light the place all right. But this is your home, not a dentist's office or a television studio. Resist the urge to overlight. Bright light doesn't make the place more cheery; it makes it more clinical.

KEEP IT LOW Distrust overhead fixtures. Pretty at best, they provide boring overall light; at worst, they give bags under eyes. Instead, use ceiling-mounted fixtures as decorative elements (with low wattage) and rely on eye-level lamps to provide most of the illumination.

INDIRECT ILLUMINATION MAKES YOU LOOK GOOD Light that passes through a material or bounces off a surface will be softer and more diffuse than a bare bulb. Reserve spotlights for objects and egomaniacs.

MAKE IT FLEXIBLE Your home's lighting should accommodate the requirements of daily life, not the other way around. Small movable lamps allow for this variety. Even the fanciest ceiling mounts are often less valuable than humble clip-ons, which let you aim them at a keyboard, bounce them off a ceiling, or spotlight treasures.

THE RIGHT LIGHT ALSO DETERMINES HOW THINGS FEEL. IT CAN RELAX, INVIGORATE, OR JUST DECORATE.

BE AWARE OF GLARE Glare is the result of strong contrast. To reduce its harshness, even out the lighting scheme. Pay particular attention to rooms with windows on only one side. Ideally, you should have windows on two sides, but you can offset the sunlight with a lamp on the opposite side.

Reducing glare is not just an aesthetic consideration. Balanced illumination makes a strong impact on the way we interact, allowing us to see the subtleties of human expression, such as a passing grin or a telling hand gesture.

Candlelight can look great *(above)*, but a few well-placed lamps *(opposite)* can provide similar warmth without smoke and dripping wax.

Now that you've pinpointed your requirements and understood the fundamental dynamics, you're ready to get to work. First, make a list of what you need. Want to read in that chair? Get a task lamp. Wish to highlight a sculpture? Consider a spotlight.

Then try it out and adjust it. Put what you've got where you need it and see what you think. If the arrangement isn't working, shift it around. The goal is to build up a balanced lighting pattern, avoiding dim corners and black shadows. Before you buy more lamps, experiment with varied wattage.

Finally, mess it up a little. The best lighting schemes are not uniform but light and dark. They give us the light and the tunnel—halos around a pair of table lamps and mystery for the less-than-perfect ceiling, a reading lamp that highlights a treasured chair and ignores a dusty computer, dappled pools that just plain look great. You can be as creative with your lighting as you are with your wall colors.

Color

Most design books tell you that everything is a snap if you are just willing to read to the end of the paragraph. But I'm going to level with you: color is not a snap. When society decorator Elsie de Wolfe advised white paint and "plenty of optimism," she wasn't kidding. Sensuous and dramatic, color can also be plain unpredictable. Part of the fault lies with physics. Since, technically, color is nothing more than reflected light, it is dramatically affected by your home's illumination.

Color need not be timid. Pick palettes that appeal to you. Trust your eye. You know what you like.

Overleaf: Most of a room's color does not come from a paint can.

Just as tricky, our tastes in color are as variable as the reality. Hues regularly fall in and out of favor. The Greeks painted rooms purple. Our Colonial forefathers preferred robin's egg blue. And Martha seems to paint every thing sage green. Individual preferences are even more exaggerated: one man's butterscotch is another's urine.

The good news is that while there are no hard and fast rules, color has some predictable dynamics. Saturated hues tend to be dramatic, pastels more calming. Reds are more exciting and blues more soothing. Dark shades tend to be powerful and lighter ones more ethereal. To promote activity, gathering places often demand deep, saturated, reddish colors, and retreats tend to be enhanced by lighter, more pastel blues. But there are exceptions. Electric blues, for instance, are invigorating and pale Tuscan reds make you want to murmur "pass the Chianti."

Color Glossary

The experts generally describe color using three variables:

INTENSITY OR CHROMA refers to a color's saturation. Fire engine red is more intense than pale pink.

VALUE describes a color's lightness or darkness. Similar in hue and intensity, cobalt blue has a greater value than electric blue.

HUE is the fancy name for color. Blue, yellow, and orange are three hues.

To more accurately describe the relationship of hues to one another, Sir Isaac Newton devised the color wheel. Look between blue and yellow, for instance, and you'll find the color made when they are combined: green.

COMPLEMENTARY COLORS, such as red and green, are found on the opposite sides of the color wheel. When used in tandem, complementary colors make a vibrant and energetic color scheme.

ANALOGOUS COLORS, on the other hand, lie side by side and produce a more harmonious arrangement.

WARM COLORS are yellow, orange, and red. Cool colors include blue, violet, and green.

TINT is the slightly rarer term for a color that has been modified by the addition of black or white.

As with all previous stages of designing your home, the key is to know what you are looking for. Before you can pick colors, you should remind yourself of the kind of room (or rooms) you are trying to create. Go back to "Asking Questions" on pages 94–97. If a cheerier entry is what you're after, pick a stronger hue. Want a sleepier bedroom? Try a softer tone. Does your home have physical characteristics to enhance or correct, like short ceilings? Use dark colors on the floor to make the room appear taller. Still not enough? Paint the ceiling a lighter value than the walls to make it feel even further away. Space too large? Rein it in with a darker color.

Pink may be the navy blue of India, but to Western eyes it can be shocking. Don't be afraid, however, to use vivid colors, even if on just one wall.

Color guidelines

Here are some simple tips for thinking about color:

LOOK AT THE ORIENTATION OF YOUR ROOMS Southern-facing spaces, as we've mentioned, get warmer light than their northern-oriented counterparts. Common wisdom dictates that you even this imbalance by using cooler tones in the south and warmer ones in the north. Uncommon wisdom advocates exaggerating the difference between rooms by doing the opposite, as in my family's home in Italy. The eighteenth-century paint job features sky blue in the sun-starved study and cooked earth in the erstwhile duchess's sun-baked bedroom. The result is *bello.*

Quick fixes

- Dark floors lift a small space by making the ground disappear.
- To make a room seem even taller, paint the ceilings a lighter color than the walls.
- Dark walls can bring the space closer, making it cozy—or claustrophobic.
- Strong color at the end of a long hallway will make it seem shorter.
- Warm hues will soften a north-facing room.
- Similar intensities will make spaces flow smoothly from one to another.
- Nighttime rooms are good places to try strong colors.
- Daytime rooms seem larger in fresh, airy hues.

CONSIDER ARTIFICIAL LIGHT Incandescent light from regular bulbs can warm up some colors and cook others. Halogens are bright and white but can flatten certain tones. Lamp shades will also play a part. A red shade on a cream wall will butter it up. On the other hand, the same crimson shade on a moss-colored surface will leave a muddy smudge.

COLOR IS MORE THAN PAINT Color doesn't just come from the walls but from objects in a room, most of which you already own. So no matter how romantic apricot walls might be in a boudoir, they'll never be restful with a blue bed. In short, you need to allow your possessions to suggest color schemes. To make an ethereal retreat, for instance, put that blue in a blue space.

WALLS *CAN* BE DULL If you want to make a dramatic color statement in a room, it is also worth remembering that it's much easier to change colorful highlights (pillows, picture frames, lamp shades) than entire walls. Don't paint these surfaces attention-drawing colors if they are in crummy shape. At the same time, recognize that painting your walls white should reflect a conscious decision, not apathy. White is a choice, and a powerful one.

Balance smaller areas of saturated color with larger expanses of more neutral tints.

Similarly, let color emerge from your home's building materials rather than from a heavy-handed "concept." I know an otherwise sane couple who decided to improve their spectacular penthouse by making it into a French château. Several months and untold

zillions later, their walls are now stone-colored, their wood floors wine-colored, and their home has all the authenticity of a stage set. Faux is facacta.

Lucky enough to have wood? Try a natural oiled finish before you whip out the paint cans. Let colors remain true to their origins and a miracle happens: the palette solves itself. Nature has it all worked out.

But you are saying, "I don't have those details. In fact, I live in a box with all the charm of an IRS auditor." Again, take a cue from nature. Go outside. If you look at the whole (the sky plus the leaves, the trees, and the stones), the sum of the colors is warm. In your home, aim for a similar balance. Use cool hues where you want, but make the environment lean toward warm and your home will feel inviting.

Basically, it all boils down to this: there is no such thing as an ugly color. Only an inappropriate one. Yes, it sounds like Oprah advice, but it's not meant to be reassuring, only truthful. Color, like the rest of design, is dependent on context. To really understand how a color will work, you have to try it out. This needn't be a multimillion-dollar investment nor entail a lifetime commitment—just a pint of your favorite paint and a good brush. Live with it for a week. See if it works. If it does, great. If it doesn't, try again. In any case, be strong. Be decisive. Don't be afraid. You know what you like.

When Picking Paint . . .

- Choose one chip lighter than the one you admire.
- Make sure you hold the chip vertically (holding it in the palm of your hand reflects the overhead light, making the color look more washed out).
- Buy a pint, test it out, live with it for a couple of days.
- Buy the best quality you can afford.

Opposite: Married no less than twice to each other, Frida Kahlo and Diego Rivera had a passionate liaison that seems to be reflected in the powerful colors of her home. Your life may not be as dramatic, but your choice of colors can be just as expressive.

Cloud, ten fingers, Rio Grande, New Mexico.

THINKING SMALL

WHAT IS EYE-POPPING WHEN YOU FLIP THROUGH A DESIGN MAG CAN BE TIRING, NOT TO MENTION EXPENSIVE, IN YOUR OWN HOME. WHILE YOUR LIVING SPACE SHOULD BE BEAUTIFUL AT FIRST GLANCE, IT SHOULD ALSO REWARD UNHURRIED HANDS AND LEISURELY EYES.

It helps if your home has good bones. Solid wood doors, generous moldings, and hefty hardware are all signs that the building was made to last. But small-scale richness is not limited to architectural details. According to *Elle Decor* design editor Margaret Russell, even the most well endowed houses need a little help. Here are some of the tricks of the trade:

"Edit," Russell advises. "To make a room photograph well," she adds, "we remove anything that clutters up the surfaces." Mail-order catalogs and half-burned candles are the first to go.

Highlight an object that strongly contrasts, either in shape, color, or material, with the environment around it: an African bowl on a glass top table, a pair of orange silk pillows on a

A HOME'S POWER COMES NOT JUST FROM WHAT IS SEEN BUT FROM WHAT IS TREASURED.

For attention to detail, few places can match the Adinath Jain Temple at Ranakpur in Rajasthan. Reached via a three-hour trek through dense jungle, the stone building is made of 1,000 white columns, each carved differently down to the head of a pin. Inch-high figures cover the ceiling, almost two stories away from the nearest set of eyes. Regardless, all of it is washed with milk each day. For the pacifist Jains, God really is in the details.

Opposite: If you've done your homework, a finishing touch, such as flowers, can help bring it all together.

natural linen couch, a couple of silver balls on a rough-hewn sideboard, a Brancusi-like pitcher on an intricately carved Indian chest.

Flowers help, of course. But so do fruits and vegetables. For a less obvious (and less expensive) decorative touch, try a bowl of pears by the sofa, where you can also eat them. For a buck more, put a dish of blood oranges on a bedside table. North Africans like to leave out platters of hard-boiled eggs and hot peppers.

The real challenge, however, is to appeal not just to a camera but to you and your guests. A great living space keeps you excited about coming home every day.

For a designer, this can be tough. After a twelve-hour day in the studio, the last thing I want to be confronted with when I get home is D-E-S-I-G-N. To maintain a sense of discovery in my own apartment, I have tried to surround myself with objects I really enjoy: a kissing manual, a thumbnail-size Bible, a stuffed goldfish. Admittedly, a little weird, but that's okay: these items may not be to your taste but they mirror my passions. They tell me stories. To reflect *your* identity, *your* choices should be different.

A collection is no more than a grouping of similar stuff. Things that may be unimportant when seen separately, look better when put together.

In your home, pay attention to items with similar resonance. Seek out the underappreciated and overlooked. One good detail—a child's first sculpture, a passport picture of an eccentric uncle, even a great old can opener—can have a significant impact, because the moment such an item is handled, the rest of your home recedes into the background. Decor becomes the context and that object the focus.

Indeed, a home's power comes not just from what is seen but from what is treasured. How you show these objects is up to you.

Some things are better left in a drawer.

Other objects, however, deserve more formal display. My stepmother, a spirited woman, collects balls and horns. Theater designer Robert Wilson has amassed over one thousand chairs. But you need not be a wealthy connoisseur to be a collector. Graphic artist Emily Oberman, for example, favors food. Along a shelf in her kitchen, Emily has assembled an array of notable food packaging, from Honor condensed milk to Pocari Sweat, an aptly named Japanese Gatorade. More everyday items offer other possibilities. Ten pairs of mittens. Twenty rolls of toilet paper. A thousand pencils. All you have to do is let yourself see.

Again, the test is passion. A dozen feeble botanical prints do not make for a compelling display. A dozen pressed leaves from your travels may.

Five Things Under $20 Every Home Could Use (More Of)

Here are five small things you can buy (and buy again) that make every home better.

1. PHOTOGRAPHS

A really good photograph is a terrific way to make a big impact with a small amount of work—and money. For contemporary historical prints (new prints from old negatives), try your government. The Library of Congress Photography Collection has over 500,000 images that focus on the United States. Collections range from panoramic photos of beauty contests to Matthew Brady's graphic depictions of the Civil War. Much of the group is available at its Web site (www.lcweb.loc.gov) and can be downloaded for free. An even more astounding bargain, however, is its custom photo lab. If you can part with an average of $30 (although prices start at $15), you can get an archival-quality print.

2. GOLDFISH

Sound a little crazy? Slightly retarded? Good. A $2 pet has a lot to recommend it. Cheery, cheap, and easy to care for, it also fulfills a more highbrow ideal: houses need to have living things to become more than vessels for your possessions. And a fish is a good place to start. Incredibly, according to a recent study by Yankelovich Partners, goldfish are also man's most soothing sleeping companions. A fish by the bedside table, they have found, is one of the most effective things we can do to insure a good night's rest. Other easy and inexpensive pets include turtles, loved by the Chinese for good luck—and good soup.

3. HERBS (LIVING)

Plants have a bad rep. To many of us, they conjure up visions of seventies' fern bars or leafless ficuses stuck in the corners of sterile studios. Get over it. Plants aren't tacky. Buy thyme, basil, and sage and put them in three small clay pots. Place on a window sill where they get plenty of sun. Herbs save you money, clean the air, smell good, and make your food taste better. They will also, as we've noted, dramatize the scale change between foreground and background. Any panorama (even a limited one) looks bigger when contrasted against something small in front of it.

4. LEMONS

If life gives you lemons, don't make lemonade. Decorate.

This citrus fruit is an inexpensive, neater, and longer-lasting alternative to flowers. They add color, aroma, and sculptural interest to any room. When they start to go bad, cut them into wedges and dry them in a warm oven (200 degrees) for several hours. Voilà. Potpourri. Dump them back in the bowls and you're in business.

5. TOWELS

Hotels caught on to this secret years ago. Nothing makes a bathroom more inviting than a heap of fluffy towels. So buy away; even the fancy stuff will only set you back about $17 apiece.

Louise Bourgeois
JOEL-PETER WIT
OLYMPIA
EFENSTAHL

A WINDOW VIEW WILL LOOK MORE DRAMATIC WHEN CONTRASTED WITH SOMETHING ON THE SILL.

Collections can consist of valuable photographs, like those at left, or of mementos of a week at the beach. It's how they're displayed that makes them special.

Once you have grouped similar things, pick a spot. Look beyond mantle pieces and table tops to otherwise dead space, like underneath a coffee table.

Pay attention to where you place these details. Photo stylists often put something big and colorful in the foreground to add drama to the picture. They learned this trick from painters who know the value of artful composition. Masterworks often lead your eye diagonally from front to back. Paco Underhill, a store design consultant to the likes of the Gap and Banana Republic, is even more specific. In the 40,000 hours of videotape he has amassed, Underhill has noted that, upon entering a room, people always look thirty degrees to the right. That's why those successful retailers always have a table right there about three steps in. A good interior need not be quite so overtly manipulative, but its details should respect this dynamic.

The foreground/background relationship also matters once you sit down. A window view, for example, will look more dramatic when contrasted with something on the sill. It can be a vase or even a plant. This detail's power also explains, in part, the

Window Nitty-Gritty

Window "treatments," as they are called in the trade, are the biggest detail in any home. If you're grappling with them, focus first on the practical. Do you want to hush a noisy street? Try a heavy drape. Or just keep out a nosy neighbor? Opt for something translucent. Do you want to preserve a view? Go with a sheer. Or block out an eyesore? Use an opaque treatment. Is the sun too bright? Too hot? Light-colored materials will help. In extreme cases, consider reflective backings. Will you ever really open and close your blinds/shades? If so, in what position do you prefer them? The basic types are:

ROLLER SHADES Inexpensive, they cut down on glare, but can be difficult to adjust and flap around when the window is open.

CURTAINS AND DRAPES Soft, with varied opacity, they insulate from sound and cold; they can also get expensive.

VENETIAN (SLATTED) BLINDS
Venetian blinds, called *persiani* (Persians) by the Italian traders who discovered them in the Middle East, are very good at keeping out hot sun while letting in air. On the other hand, they are hard to dust and the cheap stuff cracks.

OPACITY
Materials vary in their ability to block light. The three basic categories are:

TRANSLUCENTS, which diffuse bright sun but do not obscure natural light.

SEMI-TRANSPARENTS, which screen out neighbors without blocking light.

BLACKOUTS, which do what they promise and eliminate all sun.

Remember that you can layer window treatments. In a bedroom, for example, a translucent blind may hang permanently to let in light but give privacy. At night, an inexpensive roller shade behind can block out distracting glare. For total darkness, curtains or shades can be lined with a blackout backing.

continuing appeal of multipaned ("divided light" to designers) windows. The foreground mullions actually improve the vista by framing it.

In creating a display, pick objects that strongly contrast, either in shape, texture, or color, with the environments around them.

Underhill has also found that we want to touch something as soon as we come into a room. This is especially true in a room with a good interior. Details are where our tactile sense comes most directly into play. The heft of solid brass and the smoothness of burnished wood. The poof of down and the squish of pile. The rapture of great sheets. Handmade objects like ceramics

are particularly arousing to the touch. Providing more than pleasure, these imperfect objects humanize the environments we inhabit.

A peek is often more powerful than a picture window.

Some details are small in duration rather than in size. They are transient joys, like the view from a stair landing. Zen monks so value fleeting glimpses that their mountaintop retreats offer no sweeping panoramas. Instead, they avoid monotony by designing their abodes to offer passing glances of stunning views. A sliver, the monks have realized, can be much more satisfying in the long run than a picture window. So take heart, those who have found

INTERIOR DESIGN IS A SOCIAL ART, PRACTICED ON AN INTIMATE SCALE.

Inspiration

The secret ingredient in all great design, inspiration can come when you're brushing your teeth, watching a miniseries, having an argument; from a two-year-old, a noisy neighbor, your mom; from a paper clip, a stubbed toe, a bottle (or two) of wine. Newton got it from an apple, Orson Welles from a sled. Whatever the source, a good idea always makes the difference between a home you appreciate and one you adore.

themselves with just a hint of a view. A jaw-dropping vista can be spectacular, but small peeks can offer more permanent richness.

Interior design is a social art, practiced on an intimate scale. And attention to the tiny is at the core of the largest challenge: how to make a home that embodies you, a place that exists as a three-dimensional autobiography. Like any good piece of writing, it comes alive (as Strunk and White say) by being specific. You can hire someone to make pretty drawings and hammer nails, but just try finding someone who knows you as well as you do, who can tell your life story as clearly and as satisfyingly as you can. The rare designer who does is a poet—he gives form to the stuff you have always felt but could never precisely express. But you don't need to be Emily Dickinson in order to write. Your home is your story. Take it personally. ~

YOUR
HOUSE
IS
MINE

IN THE END, IT'S NOT THE SPACE THAT COUNTS BUT THE LIFE YOU LIVE IN IT.

APPENDIX A:

A REALLY GREAT SOFA

Getting that dream sofa is easy once you know how to identify quality, pick fabrics, and select a suitable style. The first thing you should know about sofas is how to tell a good one from a bad one. Focus on three factors:

Frame

The frame is the bones of a sofa. Look for ones made of "kiln-dried" hardwood. Like slow roasting, kiln-drying pulls the moisture out of the wood so it won't warp or twist later. Hardwoods, such as ash, maple, and oak, have dense grains that make for sturdy furniture. To allow the wood to expand and contract, the frame should also be glued and dowelled, not nailed or screwed. Unfortunately, metal connectors have no give and sometimes crack the wood.

Upholstery

SPRINGS

A sofa's longevity and comfort depend on its springs, which are found in the deck (the surface that supports the cushions), in the back, and in the cushions themselves. Twelve-way hand-tied coils are the best (in which each spring is secured to the frame with twelve strings). All those strings allow the upholsterer to vary the tension to allow for more support in some places and more give in others. Eight-way hand-tied versions are a solid alternative. Prefab coil units are even less expensive and can still be good. But zigzag springs are junk. Used in the cheapest upholstery, they are sinuous wires stapled across a frame. When you sit down, you sag a little and stress the frame a lot.

CUSHIONS

Contrary to popular belief, down is not best. Although they are comfortable, down pillows can swallow you when you sit down and stay squished when you get up, thereby necessitating compulsive puffing. The most expensive cushions actually have built-in spring cores (in addition to those in the frame). But for most of us, down/foam fills are a good practical choice. In these cushions, down is wrapped around a foam core, providing both comfort and stability. Surprisingly, this added labor means that down/foam can cost a little more than all down. Just make sure you're getting what you pay for. Look at the down-to-feather ratio on the hang tags (the scary ones that threaten jail for label snippers). Since the government allows a 15 percent latitude in the stated content, 10 percent down/ 90 percent feathers actually means that the filling may be NO down/ALL hard, bristly feathers.

The 100 percent high-density foam is another viable choice that can also be pretty darn nice, but the cheesy stuff is awful. It crumbles in months. One cautionary note: foam gives off carcinogenic PVCs as it ages. But take heart, almost everything will kill you faster than your sofa.

Better cushions are also lined. Because they hold the cushions together, linings reduce the stress on the decorative fabric and let it remain prettier longer. Linings also prevent errant feathers from poking through. This also means that the quality of the down is less important than it is in a comforter or pillow.

Fabric

Look for neat and sturdy tailoring. Patterns, if any, should match from top to bottom. The front of the cushions in particular should match up with the rest of the sofa.

In the $2,000 price range, many dealers will give you the option of supplying the fabric. This is called C.O.M. (customer's own material). And here's what you'll need to know:

Really expensive fabric is a great idea if you intend to admire your upholstery from afar. If you actually intend to use it, put your money where you sit and keep the fabric simple. For those of us with dogs, children, or clumsy friends, stain retardants like Scotchgard are worth the extra cost.

Solid colors and small patterns (called "repeats" by designer

THE SKETCHBOOKS OF PICASSO

$1,500 Too Much for You? How About $15?

If so, you've got to be prepared to hit the streets. Literally. Scope out the best neighborhoods in your area and find out when the big items are picked up. Be picky. Sniff first. No strange odors? OK, now look. Check to see if there are any unsightly stains, chewed cushions, or other signs of undesirable wear and tear. Still OK? Touch it. Go on. Check out the frame. I mean shake it. Bounce up and down. Hear any squeaks or creaks? If you do, move on. If you don't, put your feet up. Now all you have to do is take it away. Finders keepers.

types) can save you money since they require the least amount of fabric. Choose a style with a large repeat, on the other hand, say, foot-high sumo wrestlers, and you'll have to use a lot more fabric to cover the same area. As the average sofa requires fifteen to eighteen yards, this can really add up. Keeping it subtle also has aesthetic advantages: designs that look bold on a swatch can look downright brazen on a seven-foot sofa.

Another way to save money is to make sure you are buying upholstery goods rather than drapery, which is often sold in the same places on similar rolls. Here's how to tell the difference. Drapery fabric is narrower than upholstery goods (forty-five inches wide versus fifty-four inches wide). For every linear yard, you actually get ¼ square yard more with the real thing. Again, it adds up. Drapery fabric is also lighter, and therefore more prone to need backing to keep it from puckering and slipping.

Price

At $1,500–$2,000, you can expect hardwood construction, down seats, eight-way hand-tied springs, and, most important, a very comfy sofa that will last for years.

Style

ARMS

The most popular arm is called a scroll. It looks pretty and is as comfortable for lounging sideways as for sitting forward. A short scroll (also called an English arm) has the same shape but is pulled back from the sofa's front. The result is that there's less to bump your leg on, but also less to lean on. More mod are the square arm variations. As high as the sofa back, the Parsons arm is the most well known of this type. Low arms are often, however, the most relaxing.

BACK AND SEATS

Sofa backs and seats come in two self-explanatory variations: loose or tight. "Loose" means that the seat or back has loose cushions; tight backs and seats have the fabric pulled tautly over the sofa body. Sometimes, as with the classic chesterfield, tight backs are also tufted.

Backs can also have a lot of shapes. Again, there is not a lot of mystery here. The basic ones are straight, camelback (undulating), and rounded. High backs tend to be the most comfortable. From the side, they can either be straight or pitched. Pick a straight back because you like it or because you have to (you're set on a sofabed despite my warning), but not to save space. A pitched back will actually take less room if there's a baseboard or radiator.

CUSHIONS

Cushion styles are either "boxed" or pillow style. Boxed cushions are made from several fabric pieces sewn together: a top, a bottom, and sides. Pillows are made from just two: a top and a bottom. To add detail to a boxed cushion, you can also add a welt—piping around the edges. Some cushions have extra bumps called "tees" that wrap over the sofa arms. If a cushion tees along the back, the sofa is said to have "ears."

Some general considerations

TO SLIPCOVER OR NOT TO SLIPCOVER

Just because it looks messy doesn't mean it's comfortable. Slipcovers evoke a rumpled chic that is often at odds with the reality: the furniture equivalent of an ill-fitting sack dress. While well-made, easily removable slipcovers can be smart if you use them for what they were invented (your furniture's summer outfit: a light, washable cover for more luxurious winter wools); most of the time, you are better off with upholstery that accentuates a sofa's lines.

AVOID SLEEPER SOFAS

They make crummy beds and crummier places to sit as the mechanism takes the place of all those springs. Worse, God forbid you ever have to move it yourself; you will curse hefting around an extra 200 pounds.

DON'T BUY TOO BIG

Huge squishy sofas sound great. And great they can be if you are an NBA All-Star with an equally huge English manor house. More commonly, dream sofas must fit the smaller size of their intended occupants. For most of us, the ideal sofa is about seven feet long with low arms, a seat height of seventeen to eighteen inches, and a seat depth of twenty-three inches to the inside of the back. Any more than that and it won't be as comfortable. Any bigger than that and it probably won't fit through your door.

LIE DOWN

Sitting is not good enough. Most people don't sit ramrod straight on their sofas. They lounge sideways, often using the arm as a kind of built-in pillow. So if you really want to know whether a sofa is for you, take a load off.

Whatever your budget, remember to look for the best quality you can afford, buy what you really love, and shop with your butt as well as with your eyes. And don't forget to measure your doorways (including the elevator, if you have one) before you plunk down the cash.

Classic Sofa Styles

THE CHESTERFIELD

Tufted, same height arms and back. Manly.

THE KNOLE

Hinged arms that can be raised or lowered. Cool.

THE CARR

Tight back, loose cushions, deep rolled arms. Luxurious.

THE LAWSON

Loose back and seat, low rolled arms. Easy to lie on.

THE SECTIONAL

Pieces. Repulsive, but like many seventies' things, poised for a resurgence, which will fade as quickly as it comes.

APPENDIX B:

MAKING A HOME OFFICE

The following questions can help clarify what you need:

WHAT TYPE OF WORK DO YOU PLAN TO DO THERE? Office work? Officelike work? Paying bills requires a lot less space than making sales presentations. Are you mostly typing, reading, talking on the phone? If you work on a computer, do you need a big monitor, scanner, separate fax? For writing only, a desk can be as small as 2' x 2 ½' but scanners and faxes are such space hogs that they often need their own surfaces.

Are you sculpting or knitting? Depending on the type of work, your space needs will vary dramatically. Knitting a sweater may only take a rocker but sculpting may take a warehouse.

Are you sure you need a computer? Don't assume a home office needs a computer unless it really does. To get work done, a pencil and pad are often more valuable than a Pentium processor. Ernest Hemingway, Walt Whitman, Henry David Thoreau, Archibald MacLeish, John Steinbeck, and Vladimir Nabokov all wrote in pencil.

HOW MUCH USE WILL YOUR HOME OFFICE GET? A couple of hours a week? A day? For brief periods of time, you can borrow a regular chair and fold down an otherwise invisible desktop. If your home office is your primary business locale, it will need to be as comfortable (pick a chair that supports your back), accessible, and efficient as any traditional office.

Are you easily distracted? By the kids? The dog? The significant other? Whatever the source, if it impedes your work, stay away. Simplicity and seclusion should be your mantras.

While space and privacy needs will vary, here are some general principles:

FIND A GOOD LOCATION Look for underutilized areas, like below a stair. Bear in mind that views can be inspiring but also distracting (think of Jimmy Stewart in *Rear Window*). Pick a small space, but not a crummy one. A windowless basement, for example, can be a depressing place to work. Look for a naturally private area. Avoid the middle of the living room unless you are alone. And if you are planning to have clients over, find a spot that is as separate as possible.

CONTROL CLUTTER With small offices, clutter is your biggest enemy. Covet your desk space. Use floor lamps to avoid taking up valuable work surface. Try to keep computer equipment off your desk by hanging the CPU underneath it. If you're a slob, don't expect to reform. Make sure you provide easy storage and a quick way to clean up the mess. Organize vertically as well as horizontally. Standard desks are 30 inches high; standard ceilings are 108 inches. If you are just storing stuff below your work surface, you are missing out on a lot of potential. Again, remember to sort into daily, occasional, and once-in-a-blue-moon piles. Keep in mind that while everything needs a place, it doesn't have to be inside a soul-numbing steel file cabinet. Rolling storage is also good if it's truly portable and has a place to go.

CHOOSE THE RIGHT CHAIR AND THE RIGHT LIGHT For short periods of time (less than two hours at a stretch), opt for whatever appeals to you. Pick a chair you love. For more extended hours, use one that is tailored for your needs. To reduce eye strain, lamps should light your work surface, not your computer. And place monitors perpendicular to the sun's rays.

ADD A LUXURY Like a leather chair. You deserve it. Working at home should not feel like an uneasy compromise. Remember: a home office is a retreat. Like Saint Jerome's study, it should allow you to get away. More than a place to pay bills, this is where you go to think, to make decisions, to dream. Don't become a slave to home work. A home office should allow you to spend more time with your friends and family, not less.

MEXICO NEGRO
Self-Portrait: U.S.A.
MESA MEXICANA
Fortune

10¢
The Perfect Cigar

RESOURCES

FOR INSPIRATION AS WELL AS STUFF

Books

GENERAL

Rybczynski, Witold, *Home: A Short History of an Idea.* New York: Penguin, 1987. (See also Rybczynski, Witold, *The Most Beautiful House in the World.*) Easy to imagine but almost impossible to pin down, a great home is what we all want. This articulate architect helps us understand how.

Scully, Vincent, *Architecture.* New York: St. Martin's Press, 1994. (See also Scully, Vincent, *American Architecture and Urbanism,* and Scully, Vincent, *Frank Lloyd Wright.*) Vincent Scully, one of the preeminent architectural historians of the twentieth century, knows the effects bricks can have on the heart. By giving words to the things we all feel but never recognize as we walk through a man-made world, this passionate Yale professor brings buildings to life.

Snodin, Michael, and Elisabet Stavenow-Hidemark, eds., *Carl and Karin Larsson: Creators of the Swedish Style.* New York: Bulfinch Press, 1998. The Swedes are no slouches when it comes to design and Carl Larsson is their idol. His home, the subject of this book, is a national pilgrimage spot. It's hard not to become a fan of Larsson's ad hoc creativity and relaxed attitude toward family living. This is a seductive portrait of a happy life as mirrored in a cheerful home.

Strunk, William, and E.B. White, 4th ed., *Elements of Style.* Boston, MA: Allyn & Bacon, 1999. Why am I putting a guide to good writing in a guide to good design? Because the same rules apply.

Tanizaki, Junchiro. *In Praise of Shadows.* New York: Leete's Island Books, 1988. As this celebrated Japanese writer explains, the secret to Japanese architecture is in what's left out.

Theroux, Alexander, *The Primary Colors.* New York: Henry Holt, 1996. (See also Theroux's *The Secondary Colors,* 1998.) Not that *Primary Colors.* This trio of poetic essays on blue, yellow, and red has nothing to do with politics but everything to do with the artistic and the aesthetic, the literary and the linguistic, the culinary and the climatological, not to mention the just plain emotional dimensions of each color.

Tufte, Edward R., *Envisioning Information.* Cambridge, MA: Graphics Press, 1990. (See also Tufte, Edward R., *The Quantitative Display of Visual Information.*) Pictures can tell stories as clearly and elegantly as words. *Envisioning Information* shows us how.

Venturi, Robert, Denise Scott Brown, and Steven Izenour, *Learning from Las Vegas.* Cambridge, MA: MIT Press, 1977. (See also Venturi, Robert, *Complexity and Contradiction in Architecture.*) Because of their self-professed mystical sensitivity to form and space, architects used to think they were the products of divine selection. Robert Venturi and Denise Scott Brown changed all that by pointing out that signs and symbols are sometimes more important than perfect geometry, that what buildings communicate is sometimes more important than what they look like. Although a lot has happened in the thirty-five years since this book was first published, the message remains relevant: in order to design well, it's more important to be humble than to be graced by God.

Vitruvius, *Ten Books on Architecture.* Cambridge, England: Cambridge University Press, 1999. Written for the emperor Augustus, the *Ten Books on Architecture* is the first how-to book on design, a kind of "This *Really* Old House." This Roman Bob Vila tells what makes great places while he shows how to mix concrete. While you may not find your next weekend project in its pages, you will have fun.

Wharton, Edith, and Ogden Codman Jr., *The Decoration of Houses.* New York: W. W. Norton & Co., 1997. The famous novelist had an eye for design as well as an ear for language.

Wright, Frank Lloyd, *Frank Lloyd Wright: The Natural House.* New York: Brahall House, 1954. (See also Wright, Frank Lloyd, *Frank Lloyd Wright: Writings and Buildings.*) Frank Lloyd Wright's flair for words is almost as great as his way with buildings. And that's saying a lot.

HARDCORE

The best books by the most respected architectural theorists are engaging, provocative, and totally unnecessary for the average do-it-yourselfer.

Abercrombie, Stanley, *A Philosophy of Interior Design.* New York: Icon Editions/Harper & Row, 1990.

Bachelard, Gaston, *The Poetics of Space.* New York: Beacon Press, 1994.

Banham, Reyner, *Theory and Design in the First Machine Age.* Cambridge, MA: MIT Press, 1981.

Gideon, Siegfried, *Space, Time and Architecture.* Cambridge, MA: Harvard University Press, 1988.

Le Corbusier, *Towards a New Architecture.* New York: Dover Publications, 1986.

Mumford, Lewis, *Sticks and Stones.* New York: Dover Publications, 1955.

Norberg-Shulz, Christian, *Intentions in Architecture.* Cambridge, MA: MIT Press, 1966.

Pevsner, Antoine, *An Outline of European Architecture.* New York: Penguin, 1991.

Ruskin, John, *Seven Lamps of Architecture.* New York: Dover Publications, 1990.

Rykwert, Joseph, *On Adam's House in Paradise.* Cambridge, MA: MIT Press, 1981.

Sullivan, Louis, *Kindergarten Chats and Other Writings.* New York: Dover Publications, 1980.

HISTORICAL REFERENCE

This selection of architectural picture books shows how they did it in the old days. The purpose, however, is to inspire improvisation, not to encourage slavish imitation (unless, of course, you want to live like Louis XIV).

Brown, Frank Edward, *Roman Architecture.* New York: G. Braziller, 1961.

Calloway, Stephen, *Twentieth-Century Decoration.* New York: Harry N. Abrams, 1989.

Gere, Charlotte, *Nineteenth-Century Decoration/The Art of the Interior.* New York: Rizzoli International Publications, 1988.

Hitchcock, Henry-Russell, *Architecture: 19th and 20th Centuries.* New Haven, CT: Yale University Press, 1992.

Johnson, Philip, and Henry-Russell Hitchcock Jr., *The International Style.* New York: W. W. Norton, 1997.

Praz, Mario, *An Illustrated History of Interior Decoration: From Pompeii to Art Nouveau.* New York: Thames & Hudson, 1994.

Thornton, Peter, *Authentic Decor: The Domestic Interior 1620–1920.* New York: Crescent Books, 1993.

INSTRUCTION MANUALS BY THE MASTERS

Alberti, Leon Battista, *The Ten Books of Architecture.* New York: Dover Publications, 1987.

Alexander, Christopher, *A Pattern Language.* Oxford, England: Oxford University Press, 1977.

Fuller, Buckminster, and J. Baldwin, *Bucky Works: Buckminster Fuller's Ideas for Today.* New York: John Wiley & Sons, 1997.

Nelson, George, and Henry Wright, *Tomorrow's House: A Complete Guide for the Home-Builder.* New York: Simon & Schuster, 1945.

Palladio, Andrea, *The Four Books of Architecture.* New York: Dover Publications, 1976.

Flea Markets

How do you get your hands on a priceless gem bought for a steal? You start by looking in the right places:

eBay
www.ebay.com
Since its debut in 1997, eBay has made online antiquing a $100 million business. This all-encompassing auction has pictures of almost all merchandise and, most important, extensive dealer references to make sure you don't get ripped off. eBay is the place to go if you can't live another day without a Pan Am ashtray.

EAST COAST

Brimfield Outdoor Antiques Shows
Brimfield, MA
843-280-5834
www.brimfield-antiqueshow.com
Brimfield is the mother of all fleas. With 4,000 dealers meeting three times a year along a one-mile stretch of Route 20, it is also not a place for the faint of heart.

26th Street Flea Market
26th Street and Avenue of the Americas
New York, NY
Although pricey, this Manhattan landmark is the most well known of area flea markets. Regulars check out the less popular lots on the side streets.

WEST COAST

Rose Bowl
1001 Rose Bowl Drive
Pasadena, CA 91103
Second Sunday of every month
626-577-3100
fax: 626-405-0992
www.rosebowlstadium.com
With forty acres of stalls, the Rose Bowl makes up in size what it lacks in variety. As you might expect, old in LA is often no earlier than 1950.

LONDON

The dealers along Portobello Road are world famous and so are their prices. For bigger deals, look to less tony neighborhoods, particularly to Islington and other burgeoning areas in London's East End. Two of the best are:

Bermondsey Square
SE1 3UN
011-44-171-351-5353
Friday, 4AM–2PM
A dealer's market (i.e., "cheap"), Bermondsey has endured an unfair reputation as a place to find stolen goods. If anything, the wariness of some dealers owes more to their fear of thieves in this working-class section of London than to their suspicion of police.

Spitalfields/Brick Lane/Columbia Street
Commercial Street
E1 6BG
011-44-171-247-6590
These areas further east have refreshingly uncommercial markets with more limited selection but with the prospect of even lower prices.

Camden Passage
Upper Street
N1
011-44-171-359-9969
More an antiques area than a flea market, this Islington neighborhood is nonetheless worth a trip for the wide range of merchandise.

PARIS

Brocantes (various)
While the Marché aux Puces de la Porte de Clignancourt is Paris's most famous secondhand merchandise mart, the seasonal traveling markets called *brocantes* offer better bargains. For more information, contact one of the two main organizations responsible for the *brocantes:* Sadema at 011-33-1-40-62-95-95 or Spam at 011-33-1-45-78-98-26.

Armchair Shopping

We all need a quick fix every now and then. Here are reliable sources for decent (and, occasionally, even pretty great) stuff. Just remember: use these sources sparingly. If you buy your entire living room from Pottery Barn, it will look like it. Buy what you truly love, on the other hand, and you'll be fine.

CATALOGS

Bed Bath & Beyond
212-255-3550
This cavernous supplier is a source of the cheapest prices, not the cheapest stuff. Look past the plastic tissue dispensers and you'll find great prices on everything from Porthault linens to Wüsthof knives.

Blind Ambition
www.blindambition.com
An internet-only company, Blind Ambition maintains a large selection of window treatments at good prices.

Bludot
www.bludot.com
A Minneapolis-based supplier of hip modular storage units with terrible names (e.g., "Modelicious").

Chambers
800-334-9790
A bit pricey, but this mail-order bed/bath supplier has good quality and some unusual stuff.

Crate & Barrel
312-787-5900
www.crateandbarrel.com
Filled with sensible but often slightly soulless stuff, Crate & Barrel is a good source for a basic sofa.

Exposures Home
800-699-6993
www.exposures.com
This picture frame supplier has branched out with a furniture collection whose focus is on invention and, of course, photography.

Gardener's Eden
800-822-9600
Indoor/outdoor furniture and garden tchotchkes.

Garnet Hill
800-622-6216
Unlike other companies that pride themselves on their use of natural fibers, Garnet Hill's linens feel nothing like burlap and are surprisingly well designed. The same goes for their blankets and throws.

Herman Miller
www.hermanmiller.com
Sixteen-week waits are a thing of the past. One of the most respected names in modern design, Herman Miller now offers immediate delivery on classics like the Eames Potato Chip Chair.

Hold Everything
800-421-2264
www.holdeverything.com
Dedicated to answering the question "So where do I put my stuff?" this storage supply source has come up with some efficient, inexpensive, and pretty answers.

Home Depot
404-433-8211
www.homedepot.com
A mega-hardware-home-improvement chain not just for Bob Vila types. Some stuff, like my favorite orange metal sawhorse, is ready to go out of the box.

IKEA
800-570-4532
www.ikea.com
When IKEA first came to this country it got a bad name for supplying cheap merchandise that looked, well, cheap. In recent years, it has gone back to its Swedish roots and introduced some great design at terrific prices. More than any other place, the key to IKEA is in the edit. There are always a handful of outstanding things here; you just have to look carefully.

Knoll Quick Ship
212-334-1500
www.knoll.com
More modern classics now available without the wait.

Light Impressions
800-828-6216
fax: 800-828-5539
www.lightimpressionsdirect.com

This photographic archival supply catalog also supplies inexpensive frames. Send them the artwork and they can also frame it for you.

Linens 'n' Things
800-568-8765
www.linensnthings.com
A Bed Bath & Beyond competitor. Same pitfalls (a lot of dreck); same perks (luxury goods at low prices).

McMaster-Carr
732-329-3200
fax: 732-329-3772
www.mcmaster.com
Shh. Don't tell anybody. My secret weapon is this industrial-supply catalog, highly coveted among design insiders. Flip through its 1,500 pages and you'll find everything from Nomex oven mitts (for steelworkers) to lab furniture, as well as twenty pages on screws.

Isamu Noguchi Foundation
www.noguchi.com
The direct source for the sculptor's famous paper lamps.

Pottery Barn
415-421-7900, 800-922-5507
This ubiquitous catalog/store can be ho-hum but don't write it off. Occasionally, even Pottery Barn has some great things.

Smith & Hawken
415-776-3424
www.smithandhawken.com
Another well-known name with some unusual stuff. The galvanized metal flower vase, for example, is the same used in Paris's Marché aux Fleurs.

Smith & Noble
800-248-8888
www.smithandnoble.com
Figuring out what to do with your windows can be a chore. Offering a wide range of options in one place (wood blinds, metal blinds, curtains, etc.), at reasonable prices, and shipped in forty-eight hours, this well-ordered catalog makes it a snap. It will also send you samples if you want to see the stuff up close.

Target
800-800-8800 (to find the Target store nearest you)
www.targetstores.com
A superstore with some surprises.

Williams-Sonoma
800-541-2233
www.williamssonoma.com
At this stylish retailer, you will find everything you need for the room you probably hang out in the most, the kitchen.

Zabar's
212-787-2000
www.zabars.com
Chaotic Zabar's has many of the same things as Williams-Sonoma, only cheaper. Besides, what does Williams-Sonoma know from borscht?

Getting Rid of It

Once you've decided to get rid of the dross, now you need someone to take it away. Here are some suggestions for organizations that will not only pick up your junk for free but also give you something everyone can use: a tax writeoff.

eBay
The online auction house is as good a place to sell as it is to buy (see Flea Markets).

EAST

Furnish-a-Future, a program of the Partnership for the Homeless
Brooklyn, NY
718-875-5353

Housing Works
New York, NY
212-966-0466

Materials for the Arts
New York, NY
212-255-5924

MIDWEST

Salvation Army
Metropolitan Division

- For the Chicago area, 888-574-2587, or 312-738-4367
- For Waukegan, Illinois, and far north Chicago suburbs, 847-662-7730
- For Gary, Indiana, and northwestern Indiana suburbs, 219-882-9377
- For the Rockford, Illinois, area, 815-397-0440

Twin Cities Goodwill Industries
Minneapolis, MN
612-646-2591

SOUTH

Families Together—Family Preservation Program
Washington, DC
202-842-8666
fax: 202-842-8619

The Furniture Bank
Houston, TX
713-970-7486

The Habitat ReStore—A Division of Fort Worth Habitat for Humanity
Ft. Worth, TX
817-926-3585

Metro Atlanta Furniture Bank
Atlanta, GA 30318
404-355-8530

WEST

Goodwill Industries of Southern California (Metropolitan Los Angeles)
213-223-1211
For pickup service, call 213-222-5131

FREE the NEED
San Francisco, CA
415-587-6685
fax: 415-587-7175
e-mail: ftn@bayscenes.com

YouthCare
Seattle, WA
206-694-4500
fax: 206-694-4509
e-mail: info@youthcare.org

Magazines

Of the 152 shelter magazines available on the newsstand, here are a few of the most interesting:

Abitare
The best contemporary European design.

Elle Decor
Chic interiors.

Elle Decor (British)
New products and inventive design.

I.D.
Cool stuff.

Interior Design
A trade magazine for everyone.

Metropolis
A design magazine in an overscale newspaper format.

Nest
Offbeat but interesting.

The New York Times House & Home Section
Smartest coverage out there.

**wallpaper*
Trendy, growing stale, but still worth a peek.

World of Interiors
Beautifully printed with timeless, jaw-dropping locations.

Movies

Great movies often have great sets to go along with their great stories. Here are a few worth seeing:

Auntie Mame, 1958.
This fey favorite is cherished for its over-the-top leading lady and decor. But there's something undeniably attractive in all that camp. Maybe it's the pendant furniture.

Beauty and the Beast (La Belle et La Bête), 1946.
This dreamy romance is one of Cocteau's most imaginative creations.

The Belly of an Architect, 1987.
An architect pays the price for his design obsession.

Blade Runner, 1982.
This grim vision of a vertical city owes a debt to the drawings of Italian futurist Antonio Sant' Elia. Take *Blade Runner* as an example of how not to live.

Brazil, 1985.
A future-retro aesthetic based on a lot of tubes, which can only be fixed by Robert de Niro.

A Clockwork Orange, 1971.
Why do they call it orange when everything is white? Gleaming white. Very futuristic. Very trippy.

Edward Scissorhands, 1990.
Johnny Depp stars as a misunderstood genius whose topiary creations make him the talk of the town.

Films of Charles and Ray Eames, Vol. 1: Powers of 10, reissued in 1989.
This video collection features the remarkable *Powers of 10*, perhaps the best movie on design ever. Definitely the best film by a designer.

Frank Lloyd Wright: The Mike Wallace Interviews, reissued in 1994.
More monologue than movie, this hour-long interview features a visibly intimidated Mike Wallace talking to the ninety-year-old architect about everything from parking spaces to politics. Along the way, the irascible Wright reveals himself to be as smart and provocative as he is arrogant.

The Fountainhead, 1949.
Ever wonder what makes an architect tick? Gary Cooper stars in this story of a driven designer loosely based on the life of Frank Lloyd Wright.

Gone With the Wind, 1939.
The Old South never looked so splendid nor had it so tough.

Metropolis, 1926.
Starring Alfred Abel, this famous movie's other star is the scary/exhilarating mechanized city.

Mr. Blandings Builds His Dream House, 1948.
If you've ever felt overwhelmed by a renovation, take heart: Cary Grant has screwed it up worse than you ever will—at least in this movie.

My Uncle (Mon Oncle), 1958.
Over minimalism? You've got a friend in Jacques Tati, whose sweet comedy also manages to be a bitter indictment of modern architecture.

Sleeper, 1973.
In Woody Allen's space-age comedy, 2173 looks a lot like 1973. Period details galore (white on white, beanbags, etc.).

Triumph of the Will, 1935.
Great art can transcend politics. The proof lies in this infamous Nazi propaganda film.

2001: A Space Odyssey, 1968.
The monolith alone is enough to watch for design inspiration.

The Umbrellas of Cherbourg (Les Parapluies de Cherbourg), 1964.
Watch this for the luminous Catherine Deneuve, the entirely sung dialogue, the repainted town. Or just for the wallpaper.

The Wizard of Oz, 1939.
You're not in Kansas; you're inside the mind of a production designer gone amok.

Museums

Canadian Centre for Architecture
1920, rue Baile, Montréal, Québec, Canada H3H 2S6
(514)939-7026
www.cca.qc.ca
Created by Seagram heir Phyllis Lambert (as a young woman she convinced her dad to hire Mies van der Rohe for the company's Park Avenue headquarters), the CCA is to architecture what the Getty is to ancient art.

Chicago Athenaeum: Museum of Architecture and Design
6 North Michigan Avenue
Chicago, IL 60602
312-251-0175
www.chi-athenaeum.org
This all-encompassing decorative arts museum is dedicated to promoting the value of good design from "spoon to city."

Cooper-Hewitt, National Design Museum, Smithsonian Institution
2 East 91st Street
New York, NY 10128
212-860-6899
fax: 212-860-6909
www.si.edu/ndm
A division of the Smithsonian Institution, the Cooper-Hewitt has an encyclopedic collection of everything worthwhile in design. One of the museum's underused treasures is its 20,000-volume decorative arts library (available by appointment).

Cranbrook Art Museum
1221 North Woodward
Bloomfield Hills, MI 48303
Mail: P.O. Box 801
248-645-3300
e-mail: caa_info@cc.cranbrook.edu
Focusing on twentieth-century design, the museum is situated in a remarkable but often overlooked campus designed by Eliel Saarinen.

Design Museum
28 Shad Thames
London SE1 2YD, England
011-44-171-378-6050
www.southwark.gov.uk/tourism/attractions/design_museum
Cooler cousin of the Victoria and Albert, the Design Museum focuses on contemporary work.

The Getty Center
1200 Getty Center Drive
Los Angeles, CA 90049-1680
310-440-7330
www.getty.edu/museum
If you happen to be a French decorative arts nut, visit the exhibition galleries. For the rest of us, the Getty's real treats lie in its vaults: Walter Gropius's sketchbooks and more.

The Metropolitan Museum of Art
1000 Fifth Avenue
New York, NY 10028-0198
212-535-7710
fax: 212-570-3879
www.metmuseum.org
If the only Frank Lloyd Wright work you've ever seen is the Guggenheim, you may be surprised to realize that this arrogant genius knew so much about making a home. Back in the American wing, you will find the entire living room of the Little house, once of Wayazata, Minnesota. Ten minutes in this room and you will understand why he may be this century's best architect.

The Museum of Modern Art
11 West 53rd Street
New York, NY 10019-5498
212-708-9400
fax: 212-708-9889
www.moma.org
Until recently, the world's foremost modern museum was pretty boring when it came to design. Shunted up on the top floor, the most visible exhibition featured a permanently displayed Formula One car. Thankfully, with breakthrough shows like Mutant Materials, all that has changed.

The Victoria and Albert Museum
Cromwell Road, South Kensington
London SW7 2RL, England
011-44-171-938-8500
www.vam.ac.uk
The Victorians could be obsessive collectors, and it shows in this comprehensive museum with 4 million objects, including entire rooms devoted to such design minutiae as ceramic tiles.

Vitra Design Museum
Charles-Eames-Strasse 1
D-79576 Weil am Rhein, Germany
011-49-7621-702-35-78
fax: 011-49-7621-702-31-46
www.vitra.com
At the headquarters of the largest furniture manufacturer in Europe, visitors come to marvel at the architecture as much as to admire the chair collection. Calling on an architectural A-list, chief Rolf Fehlbaum has commissioned buildings from Frank Gehry to Zaha Hadid.

柳 幸典
MAY 23 - JULY 20, 1996
RECEPTION FOR THE ARTIST
6:00 - 8:00 PM
INSTRUCTIONS
ABC
KIDDE
DRY CHEMICAL
ABC
LOS ANGELES

Index

Photography and Illustration Credits

Every effort has been made to contact the current owners of the works reproduced in this volume.

Copyright © Arcaid: page 105
Copyright © Michel Arnaud: pages 73 (top), 137
Copyright © Bruno Barbey/Magnum: page 30
Copyright © Tim Beddow/Interior Archive: pages 58–59, 160
Copyright © Richard Bryant/Arcaid: pages 39, 44–45, 62, 163
Copyright © Robert Burke/Liaison: pages 56–57
Copyright © Matteo and Ferruccio Carassale: page 61
Copyright © Peter Cook/Archipress: page 90
Copyright © Tom Cook/Liaison: page 22
Copyright © Whitney Cox: pages 113, 141
Copyright © Jack Delano/Library of Congress: page 134
Copyright © Marc Deville/Gamma: pages 64, 104
Copyright © Eames Office: pages 78, 80
Copyright © Barbara Egan: pages 27, 120, 151
Copyright © Edmund Engelman: page 74
Copyright © Elliott Erwitt/Magnum: pages 106, 116
Copyright © Pieter Estersohn: pages 20 (right), 24, 32, 37, 43, 47, 51, 60, 81, 87, 100, 110, 121, 124, 125, 127, 149, 155, 158, 159, 161
Copyright © Everett Collection: page 84
Copyright © Gamma/Liaison: page 91
Copyright © Roger Gain/Gamma: page 132
Copyright © Gentl & Hyers/Photonica: page 157
Copyright © Porter Gifford/Liaison: page 33
Copyright © Burt Glinn/Magnum: page 25 (top)
Copyright © Richard Glover/Arcaid: page 54
Copyright © Hiroji Hamaya/Magnum: pages 166–167
Copyright © Ken Heyman/Woodfin Camp & Associates: page 18
Copyright © Todd Hido: pages 2–3, 4–5, 6–7
Copyright © T. Hoepker/Magnum: page 46 (top)
Copyright © Richard Kalvar/Magnum: pages 122–123
Copyright © Simon Kenny/Arcaid: page 114
Copyright © Shahn Kermani/Gamma: page 83
Copyright © M. Lafon/Gamma: page 46
Copyright © Carl Larsson-Gården: pages 88–89
Copyright © Robert C. Lautman: page 68
Copyright © Erich Lessing/Art Resource: page 101
Copyright © Becky Luigart-Stayner/Corbis: page 70
Copyright © Costa Manos/Magnum: page 20 (left)
Copyright © Michael Moran: page 75
Copyright © Minh + Wass: page 165
Copyright © James Mortimer/*World of Interiors:* page 36
Copyright © Martin Parr/Magnum: pages 52, 98
Copyright © Marco Pasanella: pages 73 (bottom), 86, 115, 146, 154
Copyright © Nisse Peterson: pages 88–89, 131
Copyright © F. Dewey Webster/Picture Quest: page 76
Copyright © Pollock-Krasner House and Study Center/Photo by Jeff Heatley: page 26
Copyright © Marc Riboud/Magnum: page 23

Copyright © Cesar Rubio: pages 55, 82, 129, 133, 182–183, 193
Copyright © Fernando Santangelo: page 118
Copyright © Julius Shulman: page 40
Copyright © Fernando Scianna/Magnum: pages 10, 72
Copyright © Tim Street-Porter: pages 63, 108–109, 143, 147, 150
Copyright © Schulenberg/Interior Archive: page 136
Copyright © Arthur Tress/Photonica: page 152
Copyright © Richard Waite/Arcaid: pages 34–35, 38
Copyright © Paul Warchol: pages 13, 14, 17, 66, 67, 69, 77, 102–103, 107, 126, 140, 156, 162
Copyright © Alan Weintraub/Arcaid: pages 25, 156
Copyright © Henry Wilson/Interior Archive: pages 50, 130, 139
Copyright © Andrew Wood/Interior Archive: pages 21, 42, 49, 128, 138, 142, 144–145

Acknowledgments

To my brother, Nicolas, who taught me that passion and common sense are not mutually exclusive

To Douglas Riccardi, who still returns my calls, and to William van Roden, just because

To Tibor Kalman who continues to inspire and infuriate me

To Vincent Scully who showed me that it was OK to get excited about buildings

To Andrea Au, Alexander Brebner, Amy Dana, Barbara Graustark, Heather MacIsaac, Vivek Mathur, Peter McCulloch, Peggy Russell, Isolde Sauer, Will Schwalbe, Suzanne Slesin, and Lucie Young for their savvy counsel

To Kevin Kwan for his limitless Rolodex

To Regina Ryan, my agent, who made this book possible

To Christopher Alexander for paving the way

To Jodie who has always believed in me

To Becky who tells me so every day

And, of course, to my editor, Constance Herndon, for her editorial genius, sense of humor, and lavish expense account

About the Typefaces

The text face is Minion and Minion Expert, designed by Robert Slimbach and issued in digital form by Adobe Systems, Mountain View, California, in 1989.

The captions are set in Scala Sans, designed by Martin Majoor and issued in digital form by FontShop International, Berlin, and its affiliates in 1994. Scala Sans Bold is used for heads and other text supplements.

About the Author

Marco Pasanella is a designer, writer, teacher, and photographer. His design work ranges from a rocking chair in the White House, housewares in the Smithsonian, and exclusive hotels and swanky interiors across the country. These and other projects have been documented in countless national and international publications, among them *Time, Newsweek, Esquire, GQ, The New York Times, USA Today,* and all major design magazines. Educated at Yale University, Pasanella also teaches at Parsons School of Design. He lives in New York City.